DECOY CARVING TECHNIQUES

FOR THE INTERMEDIATE CARVER

by George Barber & Larry Reader

Schiffer Publishing Ltd

Other woodcarving books from Schiffer Publishing.

Bills and Feet, An Artisan's Handbook
Blue Ribbon Pattern Series:
  Book I-Full Size Decorative Decoy Patterns
  Book II-Miniature Decoy Patterns
  Book III-Head Patterns
  Book IV-Song Bird Patterns
  Book V-Shore Bird Patterns
Waterfowl Carving, Blue Ribbon Techniques
Waterfowl Illustrated
Waterfowl Painting

Please write for our free catalog.
Box E, Exton, Pennsylvania 19341

ISBN: 0-916838-95-1
Library of Congress Catalog Card Number: 83-51212

Printed in the United States of America.
Schiffer Publishing Limited, Box E, Exton, Pennsylvania 19341

ABOUT THE AUTHORS

GEORGE BARBER

George Barber was born in Florida and raised in Charleston, South Carolina. The rich bird-life of the Carolina lowlands provided a perfect environment to develop a lifelong interest in ornithology.

George's interest in art began at age 10, when he started painting in oils. Throughout his teens he concentrated his efforts on the song birds of the Carolina lowlands.

Today George resides in Kensington, Maryland. His interest in art has broadened to cover watercolor, acrylic, and egg tempera. Since moving to Maryland, George has become fascinated with wood carvings of birds, and has developed a recognized talent in that art form. He was a contributing artist to a recently published book on duck carving and, with his wife, Bev, is also co-authoring a book on the coloration of Anseriformes.

George's art is being exhibited in galleries from New York to Florida and from D.C. to California. In addition to galleries, George has displayed his work in many wildlife art shows including those given by the Audubon Society, Ducks Unlimited, The Department of the Interior at the Smithsonian, the Ward Foundation and the Easton Waterfowl Festival. In 1982 George did a limited edition print for Maryland Ducks Unlimited (DU). In 1983 he did another limited edition for DU chapters in mid-Atlantic States.

LARRY READER

Larry tells the following story about how he became interested in carving:

"Before I reached my teens my grandfather, Joseph Reader, would fly from Minnesota to visit us during the summer. Grandpa always brought a carving knife and we would sit in the back yard and carve robins and bluejays. I have a scar on my knee to prove it. Some thirty years later I happened upon a small waterfowl carving show and had my first glimpse of realistic decoy carvings. I asked all the, 'all those real feathers' questions, bought carving books, went home, and carved a bufflehead. It did not come out too well, so I gave it to my two-year-old daughter, Caren. She colored it with crayons, so I took it back. Six months later I showed up at the Ward Competition with eight ducks and a goose."

The bufflehead Larry talks about was carved in 1977. Since then he has entered the Ward Foundation and Virginia Beach Competition shows each year. Larry has won a number of ribbons at various shows in amateur and novice categories. In 1983 he won his first professional blue ribbon at the Ward Foundation World Carving Championships with his rendition of a drake ringneck. Larry is the owner of Lawrence Reader Associates, Inc., a landscape architectural design firm in Silver Spring, Maryland. For him, carving is a form of relaxation that whiles away evenings and weekends.

Larry desired that the following statement of appreciation be included in his biography:

"I would like to thank the following people, my teachers, for their help over the years: George Walker, who, as he has for so many others, started me on my way and critiqued my ducks at every show; Don Allen, who did the smae, and is kind enough to let me assist him in teaching a waterfowl carving class each summer; Don Briddell, with whom I spent so many Saturdays in his "Ward Brothers-like" workshop in Dallistown, Pennsylvania, learning to carve and paint; and Dan Williams, who welcomes me when I persist in trying to learn his incredible painting techniques. All my ducks carry something from each of them."

DEDICATION

I dedicate my efforts in this publication to the two women in my life, my Mother and my Wife. To my Mother for her lifelong unwavering belief in my abilities and to my Wife for her day-to-day support and encouragement; no artist could have a more supportive or loving cheering section.

George Barber

I dedicate my contribution to the memory of my Grandfather, Joseph Reader, who first put a carving knife in my hand.

Larry Reader

TABLE OF CONTENTS

INTRODUCTION

Carving ducks from wood is a recognized art form which offers the carver a personal sense of accomplishment along with being a vehicle for recognition and/or a means of supplementary income. This art form has truly come into its own in the last ten years. At that time, carvers of realistic birds were far fewer than today. Art shows dedicated to this art form were equally sparse; therefore, competition was lighter. Because of the lower level of interest there also were fewer special equipment sellers and designers. This does not mean that a lower quality art was produced, but it was far more difficult to produce the quality carvings like those exhibited today.

Carvings of the mid-seventies that were hailed as realistic representations would not compare with the realism that is obtained today. To a large extent, this realism can be attributed to better equipment and, because of the greater number of carvers, to the development of countless new techniques. These techniques are what this book is all about. It is written for the specific purpose of giving the novice carver sufficient additional techniques to raise his skills to the intermediate level, assuming that there are three levels - novice, intermediate, and expert.

For years I have been exhibiting my paintings and carvings at wildlife art shows. Without exception the carvings have drawn the greatest interest. The interest normally follows the path of, ''How did you do this?'' or ''Where can I get that?'' The questioners are not only eager to receive information but equally anxious to share. If he or she knows a different way to do vermiculations or a more effective way to paint iridescence there is no hesitation to share the technique. This need to share information with the largest possible number of carvers was the driving force behind creating this book.

Bits and pieces of information, the conquering of numerous small and large problems, go toward making a memorable carving. Once you have created a carving you appreciate the fact that every square inch of your art piece confronted you with a unique problem. Applying various techniques helped you solve those problems. With that idea in mind, Larry and I have concentrated on describing the techniques we have used to solve such problems. Even though the presentations are geared to discussing a project, they are not intended to tell you how to do any specific piece. The value of this book comes in applying the techniques of the professional artist's presentations to any bird carving, whether it be waterfowl or other birds.

In using this book you should understand that our techniques, specifically those in the project chapters, are to a large extent dictated by our goals. It may come as a surprise, but it is not the goal of every carver to produce the perfect carving. I use the word ''goal'' to mean the principal reason the artist produces carvings. If the goal is winning ribbons, then production time is not a major factor, and some of the techniques may be extremely time-consuming. On the other hand, if supplementing an income is the artist's goal, then time is a principal factor, and the techniques are geared accordingly. Our goals encompass both of the above, and, as you will see, our techniques differ accordingly. This diversity of interest and approach should provide a broad and interesting spectrum of techniques to cover your needs as a carver.

To make this book more useful to the carver, we have included a list of retailers who carry the equipment you will need. We have also included a chapter on marketing your art. Even if your goal is winning blue ribbons, there is nothing wrong with realizing some additional income.

Larry Reader is the author of the section on competition carving. George Barber has written the remaining chapters and this introduction. No attempt was made to resolve apparent contradictions between the authors of the project chapters. The differing techniques and opinions of the authors will allow the reader to experiment with various methods and choose those which are best suited to his own style and purpose.

I would like to thank Bill Fisher of Gaithersburg, MD, a good friend and fellow carver, who took the time and effort to read and comment on this manuscript. His contribution is greatly appreciated.

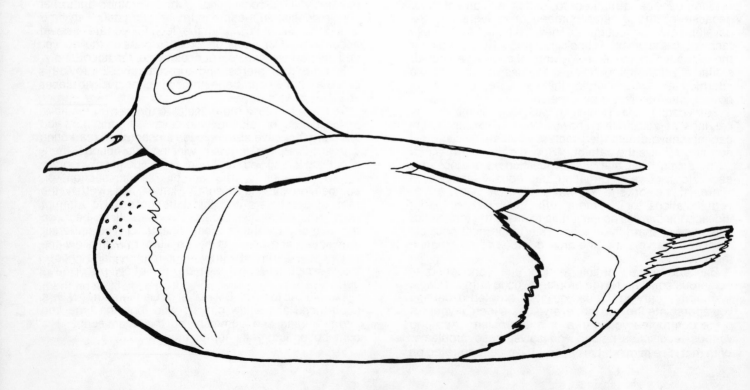

NECESSARY TOOLS, EQUIPMENT, & SUPPLIES

A discussion on tools, equipment and supplies can be a never ending dissertation. There are many varied items the carver can purchase to support his art. The variety is limited only by the imagination of the artisans, who for the most part are the creative force behind old and new designs. It is an easy and inviting trap to ramble on about the unique and innovative items available, but such a discussion is not in keeping with the objective of this book, which is to upgrade the novice carver to the intermediate level. This chapter will cover only items that the intermediate carver should have to better control the creative process and produce a higher quality carving.

The degree to which a carver can control any process is to a large extend related to the tools, equipment and supplies used. For example, you can complete a carving with only one knife, including hewing the block to form a blank, relief carving the details of feather structure, and carving crevices. Your control over each function would vary with the size and shape of the blade and the angle and size of the cut. Knives come in all shapes and widths. If you have small, medium, and large blades of various angles, each designed for a specific cut, your control over each carving tehcnique is greatly increased.

I have divided this writing into three basic areas: (1) tools, specifically hand tools; (2) equipment, power tools and other non-tool items; and (3) supplies, those items of which the carving is made. Obvious items normally found in the workshop are not covered. Also, this list is not exhaustive. If you have found a special tool that serves your purposes, by all means use it, and let me know about it so in the first revision of this book I can tell others about it.

Tools

I used the knife as an example. Without question it is the most basic of tools. By now you should have at least two knives; a small blade for detail carving and a medium blade for heavier work. To gain more control in actually carving the wood, I would recommend purchasing a knife with a small blade at approximately a 45 degree angle, and a medium size blade in the shape of a "J". The angle blade is most useful around the flank section and the "J" is useful at any high point a flat knife can not reach that you need to lower; for example, between the scapulars in the middle of the back. Gain some experience with these new additions before adding more blades to your tool chest. It is extremely easy to wind up with far more knives than you can use. Tool costs are so high it is prudent to purchase only what you need, and add only that which you can associate with a specific technique. If both criteria are not satisfied, do not buy the tool.

Files are also basic tools. At this point, you should have at least a basic set of "jewelers files" or "needle files." These files come in fine, medium or coarse. The novice should have at least one set of the medium. For greater flexibility, consider adding a set of "rifflers". Rifflers are odd shaped files used around bills and other irregular areas. Rifflers add a versatility that is impossible to achieve any other way. If you have never used them you have a pleasant surprise in store. You can purchase small rifflers (See retailer's list).

Wood chisels are items the novice should add to his art bin. The basic set of six will consist of straight blades in three sizes; several gouges; and a "V", or parting tool. The size of the set should be chosen carefully to match the size of your carving.

Sharpening tools is more than a bothersome task; it is a vital function. The usefulness of all cutting tools is directly related to the ability of the carver to keep them razor sharp. First, do not purchase leather sharpening wheels: wheels that are made of layers of leather which fit on a grinder. Such wheels have a tendency to gouge the blade unevenly rather then stropping it evenly as a flat leather strop will do. A flat leather strop, honing oil, and abrasive powder are the essential items for keeping a knife, sharp. If your knives need more than stropping, I recommend that you take them to the next wildlife art show and have a professional put an edge back on them. Once you have a good edge, keep it by stropping it after every 10 to 15 minutes of use.

An odd item to find in the area of tools is duck bills. That is correct, duck bills. You can not cut, carve, sand or grind with a duck bill, but in today's hectic competition the duck bill is a necessary tool. The bills I am referring to are, of course, cast duck bills. They can be cast either in lead or resin. I prefer the latter because of its lighter weight and lesser cost. The bill is one of several "soft parts" of a duck. After death, the bill will shrink; sometimes as much as 50%. If you have a mounted duck, compare its bill to a cast bill. After the comparison, there will be no doubt about the need for this tool.

There is a variety of other small hand tools one can acquire. Unless your resources are unlimited, I would suggest adding to your tool box slowly. Even after you have decided to buy, shop around to find the lowest price. It is not uncommon to find the same item being sold by a number of dealers, with as much as thirty percent difference in price. I would not advise purchasing knives or crafted items, like bills, with price as your main criterion. The quality you are assured by buying from a dealer you know to be good outweighs the money you save by purchasing the item at a discount from someone else who might sell you an inferior product.

Equipment

Under this heading I have included electrical and heavy equipment. The electrical tools used for burning feathers are specially designed burners. These burners first appeared in the seventies, and were designed by carvers. If the novice does not already have such a tool, then it should be one of the first additions to your work bench. I use George Walker's Feather Etcher (see Producing a Saleable Carving).

The Foredom tool is another of the basic tools. This tool adds considerable versatility and speed to the artist's ability to shape the wood. Even though this tool is very desirable, it is not necessary. World class birds have been produced without it. Still, there is no denying its desirability.

Shop tools, such as bandsaws, table saws, planer-jointer, power sander, drill press, drum sander, etc., are all desirable, but few are necessary. If I could only have one piece of power equipment it would be a drum sander. You can purchase one for about $500.00, or you can make one for about $25.00. It would be misleading to say that the homemade model performs as well as its commercial counterpart. It does not. Still, it does the job at a considerably lesser cost. If you decide to do the latter, which is what I recommend, you will need an electric motor, a sanding drum and an arbor to connect the drum to the motor.

All of this equipment is readily available. The motor I use is twenty years old. I picked it up at a yard sale for $5.00. If you can not find one locally, look in the telephone directory under junk yards and used motors.

Purchase the motor, a sanding drum, a sleeve for the drum, and an arbor of the correct size. The size of the latter pieces of equipment is dependent upon the shaft size of your motor. It will be obvious how the drum sander should be assembled once you have the equipment in hand. After assembly, bolt the motor to a work bench. When using this or any other power equipment, be careful. If you jam your hand on the sanding drum, it will sand the skin off your hand before you realize what has happened. Never apply force in a

direction that would carry your hand, arm, or body into the drum if you should slip.

This tool produces fine "saw dust" by the mounds, so use a breathing mask to prevent inhaling the dust; the same holds true when you are using the Foredom or any grinding tool. Also, with this and any power tool, wear eye protection. Take all of the standard safety measures power tools require; you will be the benefactor.

The sanding drum gives you the capability of rapidly producing a "blank" (the foundation carving) from a piece of wood. Blanks are also available from numerous suppliers. Even though you carve your own blanks; it is a good idea to have a good professional blank available for proper size and proportion. Simply put, the professional blank becomes a tool, just like the resin cast bill.

Supplies

I have included painting supplies and other items under this category.

By now you should have the basic brushes and paints. My principal medium is acrylics; therefore, my recommended supplies are geared toward the use of that medium. Make sure that your brush box contains some fine (1, 0, 00) red sable brushes, 3, 4, and 5 black sable, and some larger white fiber brushes.

You should also have a "color wheel", such as Grumbacher's "Color Computer", to give you a basic idea on mixing a variety of colors. For the purpose of mixing and retaining a quantity of paint for use over the period of weeks it may take you to paint a duck, obtain some small plastic vials or bottles. This is critical, especially if you are using a "tempera" technique in painting. (See Painting Techniques.) For the purpose of blending acrylic shades by the stipple method (see Painting Techniques), add sponges to your art bin—both wool and finger sponges. (One gives you a fine pattern, the other a coarse pattern)

FEATHERS

Most carvers do not have a detailed knowledge of feathers and their structure. Such knowledge, while being desirable, is not vital to the intermediate carver. It is more important to have an understanding of where feathers grow, and in what patterns.

Feather Tracts

If you have ever seen a thoroughly soaked bird, you may have noticed that it appeared to have bald spots over certain areas of its body. The reason for this appearance is that its principal or "contour" feathers (i.e., feathers other than down that form the outline of the duck) grow in certain tracts (more correctly in numerous lines) over its body. The location of these lines or tracts determines the name of the tract. An understanding of feather tracts will help you appreciate why feathers lay the way they do, and give your carving a more realistic look.

Figure 1 represents a plucked duck with the feather tracts represented by rows of black lines, this is a simplified diagram. The names of these tracts are, (1) capital tracts, (2) spinal tracts, (3) humeral tracts, (4) femoral tracts, (5) crural tracts, (6) ventral tracts, (7) caudal tracts, and (8) alar tracts. More meaningful names for these tracts would be (1) head tract, (2) upper back tract, (3) shoulder tract, (4) thigh and lower back tract, (5) lower leg tract, (6) side and belly tract, (7) tail tract, and (8) wing tract.

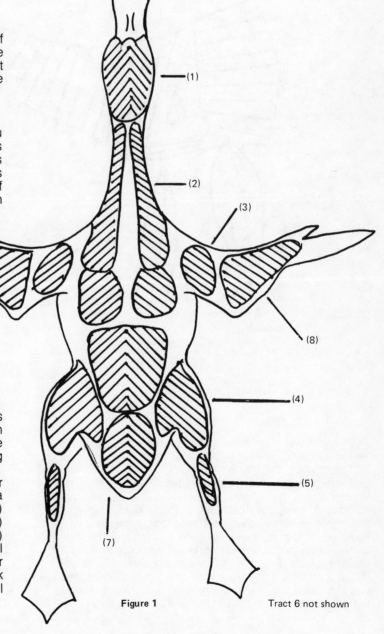

Figure 1   Tract 6 not shown

Here is an example of how the knowledge of feather tracts can be of use to every carver. Principal groups of feathers, such as the tertials and scapulars, are prominently displayed on waterfowl carvings. Scapulars grow from the shoulder tract (3); therefore, they must radiate from that location (see figure 2) with the scapulars overlapping the tertials when the wings are folded. In the folded position, the feathers are staked with the outermost primary on the bottom and the scapulars on top. Therefore, the least visible feathers are the primaries; you can see their tips extend from under the tertials. On some species you can see the edges of some primaries up to the secondaries. Still, the most visible feathers are the scapulars and tertials.

that matter, where to position feathers. I have seen some odd looking mounted ducks, including ones I have mounted myself; I am not a great or even good taxidermist. Photographs are far more accurate. There are many available. You can find them in numerous books, and many photographers sell them at shows.

Contour Feather Structure

To continue our discussion of feathers, let us look at the basic structure of a contour feather. As stated before, the contour feather is any principal feather other than down that forms the outline or contour of the duck. The shapes of these feathers vary with the type of duck, so it will be necessary to examine mounts, study skins,

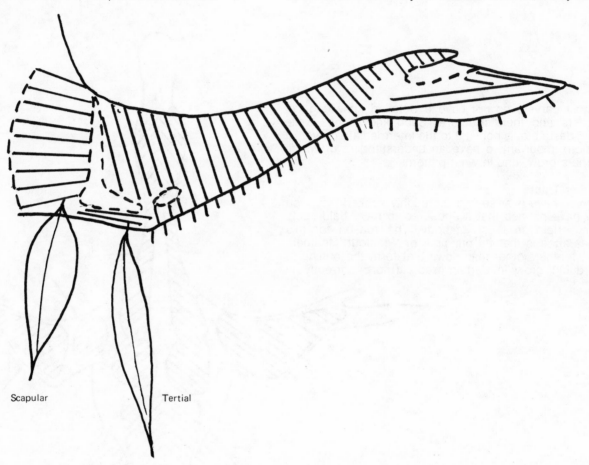

Scapular   Tertial

Figure 2

Figure 3 will give you a graphic view of some of the feathers that grow in the various tracts; the numbers correspond to the particular tract. Some tracts have feathers of various shapes. Figure 3 only shows one feather from each tract. Knowing the approzimate number of principal feathers that the duck has is as important as knowing where they grow; especially when you are trying to decide how many secondaries to show, or how many primary tips to make. If you are striving for realism, study photographs, which are available at your library, so that you represent the correct number. I caution you against using mounted specimens to make the determination on how many primaries to show or for

or detailed photographs to determine the exact shape of the feather for your carving. Regardless of the shape, the structure of the contours are the same. Each has a center shaft or rib with a vane attached to each side.

The vanes are made up of individual barbs, which are plates that are interlocked. The angle of the barb to the shaft becomes smaller as you work from the base of the feather to its tip. Also, the opposite end of the barb (the end away from the shaft) curves more than the remaining portion and, of course, curves toward the end of the feather. Utilize this information by rolling or slightly turning your burner handle when burning the barbs.

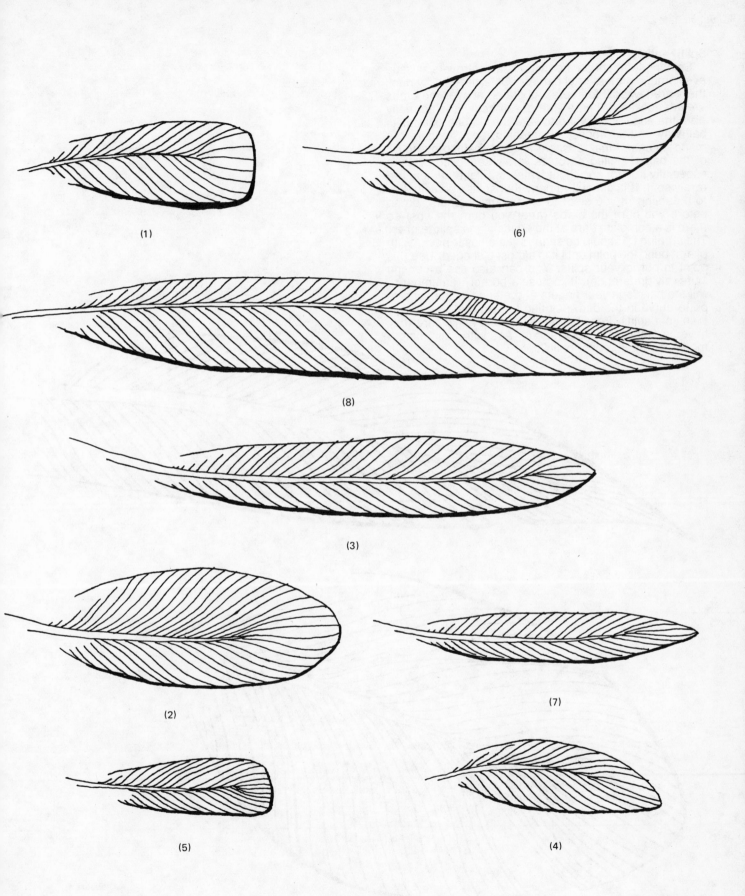

(1)

(6)

(8)

(3)

(2)

(7)

(5)

(4)

Figure 3

Split Feathers

Splitting feathers on a carving is a controversial issue even among professional carvers. On a healthy dry duck there are few split feathers. As stated above, the barbs are interlocked. When a split does occur, it is normally from the edge of the vane toward the rib one-quarter to half way. In the process of preening, split feathers are made-up again; that is, spear shaped shafts growing off of the barbs, called barbules, are interlocked. This is especially true for non-flight feathers. Flight feathers are rarely split. It is difficult to deny that splits add esthetics to a carving. If you elect to split some feathers, do so before you burn the barbs (after you burn the ribs) so there is a complete barb at the edges of the split feather. The burning tip should be shaped like a spear point. With pliers, bend the point until it is almost L shaped. Use this point to put in your splits. You can also use a carving knife (my preference). If you use a burner, remember to roll the handle in your fingers at the edge of the vane to put a curve in the barb pointing toward the feather tip. Plan your splits. Pencil them in first and make sure they have a random appearance. As with all things, moderation is the best policy.

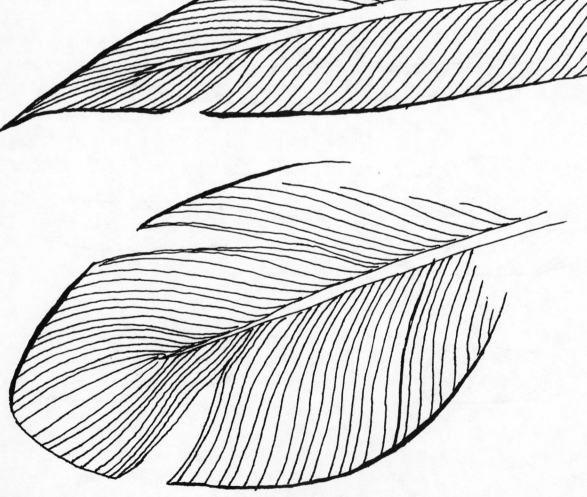

Figure 4

16

PAINTING TECHNIQUES

This section is devoted to acrylic painting techniques. In the projects sections, Larry and I refer to these techniques.

Like any medium, acrylic painting has pros and cons. One disadvantage, which may be perceived by the oil painter, is its rapid drying time. Normally, one would think that its short drying time would be welcome. By most acrylic painters, it is. Still, the rapid drying time makes it difficult, if not impossible, to smoothly blend from one shade to another by flowing the paints together. Since shading is a principal factor in the success of a painting or carving, techniques must be mastered to accomplish the gradual change from one hue to another.

Changing of shades can be accomplished by washes; stippling; tempera techniques; dry brushing; working quickly with wet in wet washes; or adding retarder to slow down drying, then blending the colors.

Washes

One of the big advantages of acrylic paint is that it can be laid in a thin wash, in which the color is so diluted that only a hint of color shows up on the object it is painted on. A series of these washes laid one upon the other, with incremental boundaries toward the darker shade, is a common method for blending with acrylics. Its disadvantage lies in the time to produce the number of washes needed and, even though they are barely visible, the distinct boundaries of each wash.

Stippling

If you have ever looked at a newspaper picture under a magnifying glass, you know what stippling looks like. You take a small brush and make a series of dots with the very tip. The dots should be all the same size. The color and density (number of dots per given area) will determine the shading. You can also stipple with sponges. I recommend that you experiment. You will be amazed at the variety of patterns that can be created. This technique can be used to simulate fine vermiculations. Take a fine sponge (a finger sponge) and load it with one hue darker gray than the base coat. Lightly touch the surface to create the pattern. Do not overdo it. Let it dry, examine, then go over it as needed.

Tempera

Egg tempera was the acrylic of the Renaissance era. The method of painting was to use small brushes and tiny strokes. The same technique can be used with acrylics. The result is an almost photograph quality. The disadvantage lies in the enormous amount of time needed to produce the painting.

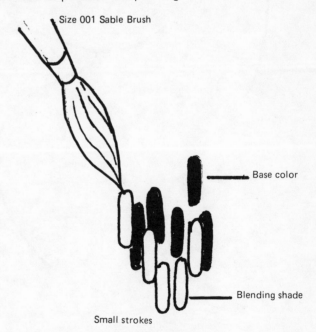

Size 001 Sable Brush

Base color

Blending shade

Small strokes

TEMPERA TECHNIQUES

Figure 5

Dry Brushing

A dry brush means that there is insufficient paint in the brush (this mixture can be thick with color or thin) to allow for an even flow or line to be drawn; in fact a broken line would be drawn. With this technique you dip your brush, then fan it out against your pallet. While it is in a fan shape, draw the brush against the pallet until the paint is coming off irregularly (in broken patches). This technique is used on top of a base coat and with thin (a little color mixed with a lot of water) color for the illusion of vermiculations. To achieve the desired color for shading it may be necessary to go over the area several times.

Conventional Blending
Using water color techniques, if you work quickly, you can blend the edges of two wet washes. Still, no matter how skillful you are, when you use acrylics there will be a slight or rough border line.

Acrylic Retarder
You can purchase a drying retarder and add it to the acrylic. This helps by allowing you time to "work" or brush the boundaries of two colors together. In my opinion, this application should be limited. If you are depending upon retarders then I would recommend using oils, since that is the technique you have developed.

Graded Wash
Using the above techniques (stippling, tempera, dry brushing or blending) you can lay a graded wash for the foundation and then paint your pattern on top. For example, a widgeon's head is a graded wash of gray upon which you lay very dark gray spots.

Scrubbling
This is a technique of random brush strokes back and forth. I use it to lay a foundation color.

COMPETITION CARVING

OF
REALISTIC DECORATIVE DECOYS
BY
Larry Reader

I would like to emphasize that the following is a description of how I carve a duck. It is not necessarily the way you will carve. We all take some ideas from a person and discard others. Few of my techniques are my own. They are composites learned from other carvers, personal friends, and Ward Foundation classes (usually offered each spring at their Ocean City show).

Just as I do in my office work, I keep time sheets on all the ducks I have carved. It seems that my most recent carvings have taken more time than my early ones. It is interesting to note that I have carved an average of 135 hours for every ribbon I have won. That means that many of my ducks have not won any ribbons. The average duck takes me sixty to eighty hours to complete. For example: a mallard hen took me 34 hours to carve, 13 hours to burn, and 28 hours to paint; a merganser hen took me forty hours to carve and burn and nineteen hours to paint; and, a ringneck drake (full bodied with

feet) took 55 hours to carve and eighteen hours to paint. Generally I find the hens take longer to paint than the drakes, even when vermiculations are involved (drakes like the mallard, widgeon, gadwall, and redhead).

The Beginning

The first step after picking the subject is to research the duck, using mounts and photograhs. Sketch and change the posture from that in the photograph until you are satisfied with the profile, and then draw the profile to scale. There are many books that give nominal size (the average length from front of breast to tip of tail). The mount is of some help, but mostly in the color area. The mounted bird skin may be stretched and the frozen bird will be dehydrated, hence smaller than normal, so I prefer photographs, a nominal measurement, and the bill size.

The Pattern
My first drawing is one of many before the pattern is finalized. Draw a profile and set it aside for a while.

Figure A-1 ROUGH IDEA SKETCHES FROM PHOTOS AND BOOKS

Then, with tracing paper overlays, begin drawing and redrawing the head in different positions. When it is the right shape, including the bill detail, overlay it on the drawing of the body. Tilt it up and down, and raise and lower it until you find something in the attitude you like. Work with the drawing of the tail area in the same way, raising and lowering it until you can trace one composite drawing from the many pieces of paper. The time spent at this stage will be reflected in the quality of the carving. The hours spent in research and planning are the most important ones in relation to the total time it takes to do a carving.

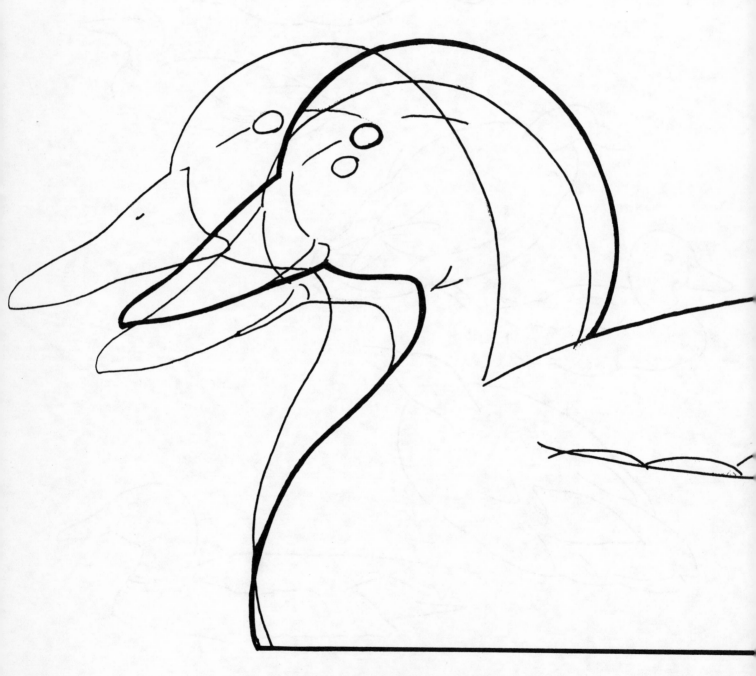

Figure A-2 SKETCH PROFILES

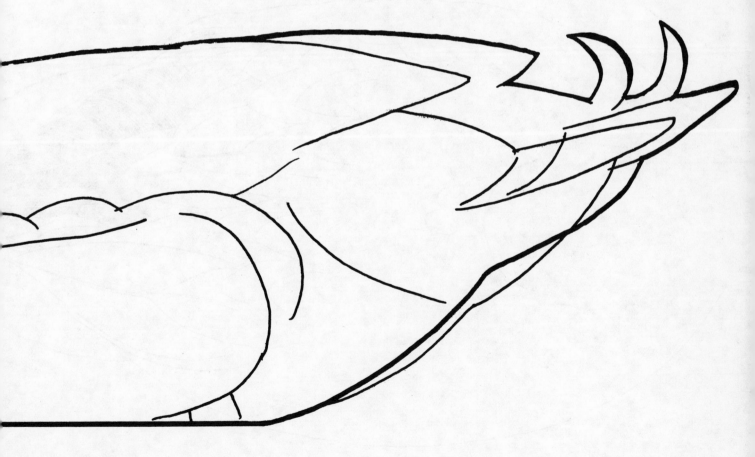

The mounted or frozen bird is most useful in determining widths, lengths, and general shapes of the different feathers. All of this information is sketched on a sheet for use in laying out the top view of the duck and during carving.

Figure A-3 TERTIAL AND PRIMARY LAYOUT AND BURNING

Figure A-4 PLAN OF TERTIALS AND PRIMARIES

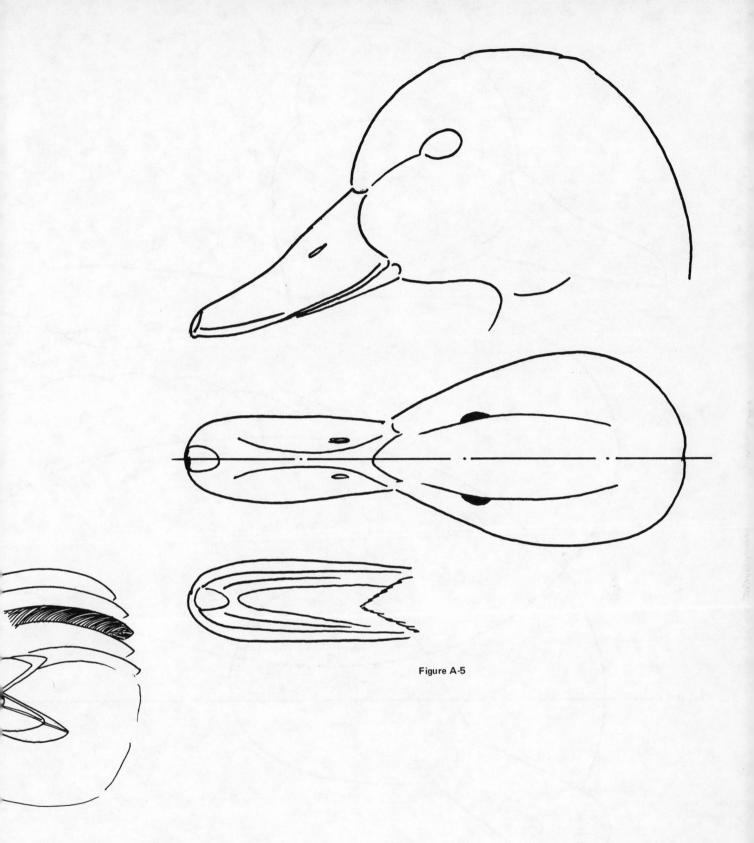

Figure A-5

The top view will show the spread of the tail feathers, width of the body, layout of the tertials, and angle and width of the head and bill.

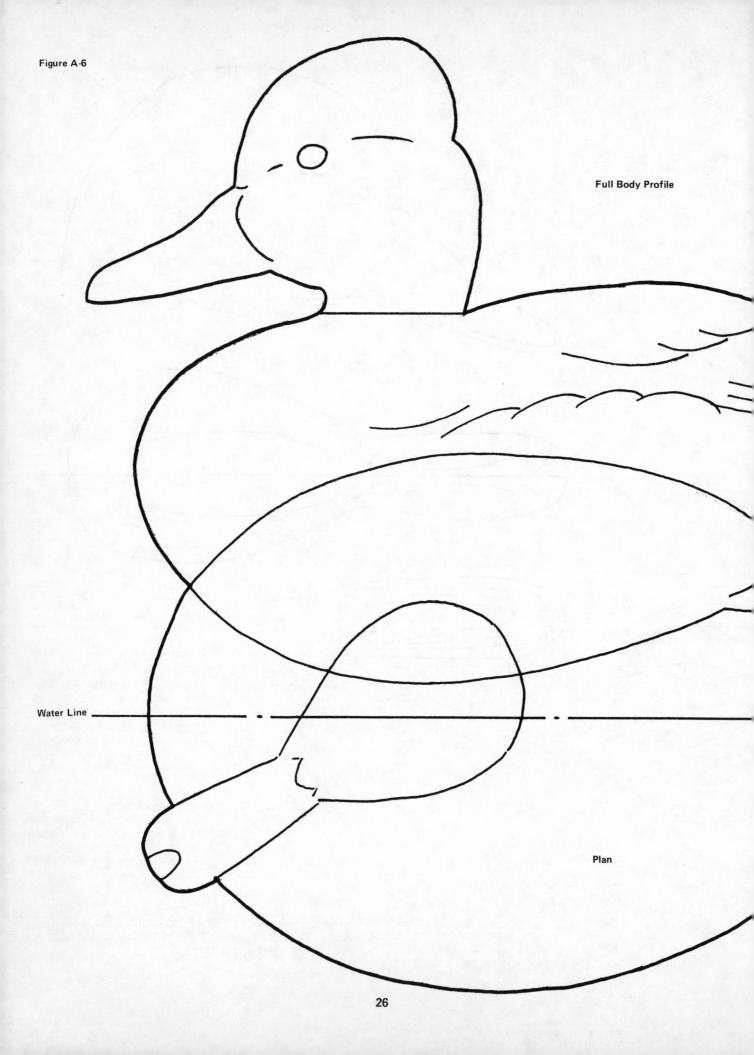

Figure A-6

Full Body Profile

Water Line

Plan

26

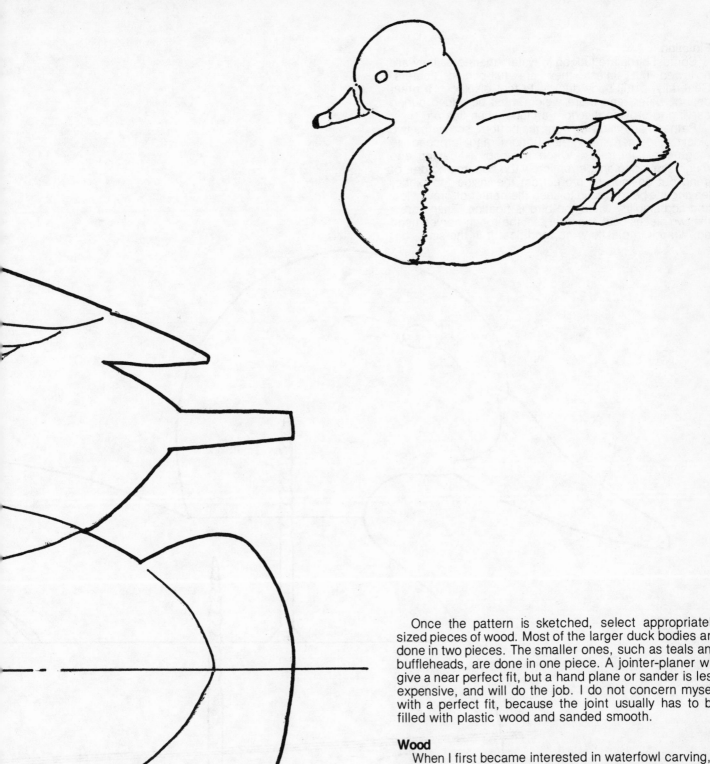

Once the pattern is sketched, select appropriately sized pieces of wood. Most of the larger duck bodies are done in two pieces. The smaller ones, such as teals and buffleheads, are done in one piece. A jointer-planer will give a near perfect fit, but a hand plane or sander is less expensive, and will do the job. I do not concern myself with a perfect fit, because the joint usually has to be filled with plastic wood and sanded smooth.

Wood

When I first became interested in waterfowl carving, I had no tools, so I went to the local hardware and bought a piece of 1x8 inch pine and a coping saw. I cut, stacked, and glued four pieces together for the body and three for the head. From this foundation I carved a bufflehead, knots and all. Some time later when I had finished a full-size goose, I decided it was time to break down and purchase a bandsaw and some basswood. I now use basswood because of the lack of grain, relative softness, and what I call "carveability" of the wood. I have found that the lighter colored wood is also lighter in weight, less dense, and easier to carve.

Flotation

Contest birds are judged in water; therefore, they are hollowed out unless they are full-bodied floaters. Generally, a full-body duck with feet displaces a great deal of water, and more weight must be added during carving to provide the right attitude when floated.

Rather than hollowing from the bottom, screw the two blocks together from the bottom and proceed to rough-carve the duck. When the body is carved and rough-sanded to shape, unscrew the bottom and drill or grind out an inch or more from the inside top piece, leaving the bottom solid to keep the center of gravity low and add stability when the bird is floating. Then screw the two pieces back together, set the rough-carved head on, wrap it in plastic wrap, and float it in the sink.

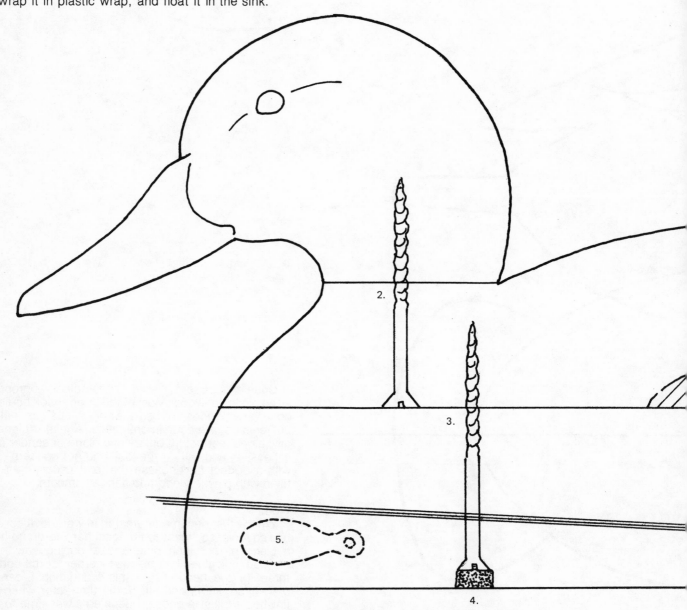

Figure A-7

28

1. Hollow out top, and bottom if necessary.

2. Glue and screw head on to top body block.

3. Glue and screw top and bottom body blocks together.

4. Fill screw holes with plastic wood.

5. Add weight in front if necessary.

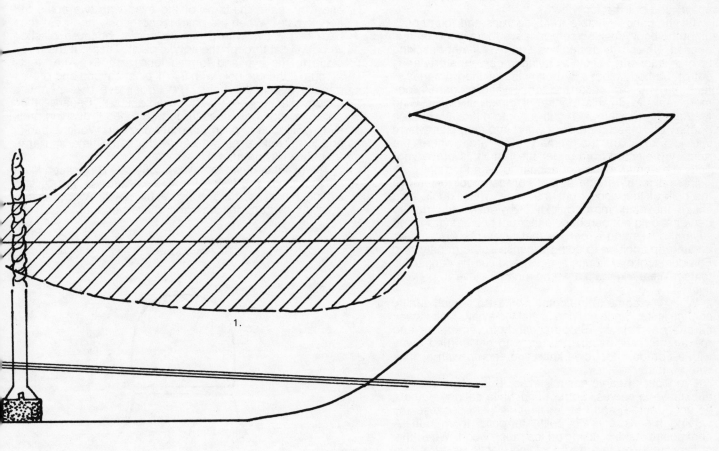

1.

If the carving floats high, add a fishing weight in the bottom half. If it floats low, hollow more wood out of the top, and possibly a little from the bottom. This procedure of floating, hollowing, and refloating takes time, but the first birds out of the contest tank are always the ones that do not float correctly.

When the duck floats well, glue the weight, making sure it is embedded in wood and will not come loose. It is now time to join the top and bottom with Elmer's Carpenter Glue, countersink the screws, and fill the countersink with plastic wood. Never use epoxy to join the blocks. Seal the bottom with four or five coats of gesso.

An alternate method of hollowing is to glue the blocks together before carving, hollow out from the bottom after rough carving, and add a wood plate to the bottom. In either case, it is necessary to float, hollow, and refloat until the balance has been achieved.

Rough Carving

My first decoy was done with a coping saw and a carving knife. I now use a bandsaw, planer, grinder, Foredom tool, Dremel, knives, chisels, and wood burners.

Begin by cutting the profile of the body along the outside edge of the pencil lines transferred from the pattern. Nail the top piece, which was cut away, back on again; and cut the top view.

Tilt the bandsaw table to 45 degrees and round off a bit of the body, making sure to leave more wood than is needed. Unless my design has a primary feather sticking up high in the air, I begin by trying to carve the primaries out of the body block. By beginning at the primaries, I feel that you can make the tertials and primaries look more realistic. In this manner, I make all of the wing feathers flow together. If you run into difficulty, cut the primary off. Insert a piece of wood into the place where you just removed the primary. The area where the primary projected from under the tertials is precarved. Thus the primaries do not appear to be added on.

I use a rotary grinder and a Foredom tool to remove the bulk of the wood from the body. These tools help shape the duck more quickly. Obviously, the novice carver should not purchase either until he has produced several ducks and is certain that he wants to continue carving. In addition to being expensive, the grinder and Foredom tool make quite a mess, and can be dangerous to use. Wear a good mask and a chain glove to prevent injury.

When you come to the detail work, use a good quality carving knife. Since carving is "taking away," take away carefully and slowly. Stop frequently to remeasure and reevaluate the carving. It is easy to get carried away with a Foredom tool or a knife and end up with a duck with no tail.

Every duck I carve has mistakes. This is true of every duck anyone carves. Some I find while carving. Others go uncorrected, and I never hear of them because my carving friends are too polite to point them out. A common mistake is taking off too much wood. When this occurs, rebuild the area by adding plastic wood in thin layers. It sands well, but has a tendency to pit. Burning the plastic wood can only be done with a cool tip.

The Head

The head gives the duck personality. Bill detail, eye location, size, and width are very important. After cutting the profile of the head, drill a very small hole thru the eye location with a drill press while the head is still in block form. This 3/32'' hole acts only as a guide, because the head shape may change slightly during carving, thereby shifting the eye. This symmetrical hole in the general area is very helpful in determining the final location of the eyes. Try to take great care in locating the eyes. I once overheard a judge remark that my green winged teal looked like a woodcock because its eyes were so far back. The depth of the eye and the width of the head at that point are important factors. In most of my early duck carvings, the eyes were too far apart. I now try to concentrate on preparing the area around the eye holes. The distance from one side of the head to the other at the eye should be just a little wider than the bill.

Drill the eye hole with a speed regulated Foredom Tool for more control. Drill the eye hole slightly larger than the glass eye being used. I generally use a glass eye which is a size larger than normal. The larger hole permits me to move the eye, and the larger glass eye allows me to cover part of it, which prevents the startled, round-eyed look.

I purchase uncolored glass eyes on wire. After matching eye sizes and pupils, which are rarely the same on one wire, paint the back of the eyes with two coats of acrylic paint. When the paint is thoroughly dry, coat the back of the eye with 5-minute epoxy, because plastic wood will eat through the acrylic paint. Then cut the wire close to the eye and form a loop or hook. After test fitting, fill the eye hole with 3 in 1 plastic wood and press each eye into the hole. The larger eye hole permits excess plastic wood to squeeze back out. Because the small location hole goes through the head, pushing one eye in will tend to push the other one out. Working back and forth, both eyes are set at the same time and are (hopefully) symmetrical.

The exact depth of the eyes is critical. Try to keep just a slight glass arc visible from the front. As you finish setting the eyes, scrape the extra plastic wood away from the eye and let the carving sit overnight.

Figure A-8

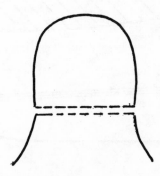

Small location hole drilled thru.

30

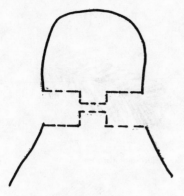

Holes drilled larger than eye.

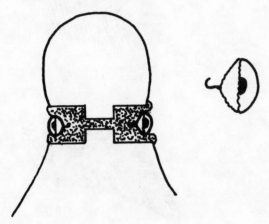

Fill eye holes with plastic wood and insert eyes.

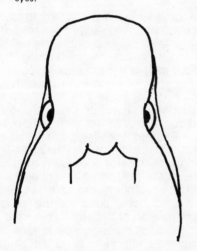

Let plastic wood dry, then form area around eye with plumbers putty.

Next add a small amount of plumber's putty, which softens with water and is finely textured, to the edge of the eye. Using an old wet paint brush, form the eyelids, and the area around the eyes. This is your last chance to match the location, shape, and size of the eyes.

When the putty has set, paint the eyes with 2 or 3 coats of gesso to protect them from scratches.

Carving the Bill

When carving the bill it is important to keep the center line established from the nail to the tail. The bill must be symmetrical. Carve the bill close to final form with a knife. After sanding, use a burning iron and small chisels to form the details. It is important to keep the bill narrow where it joins the head, rather than flaring it out to meet the head. Cast bills are a great help in carving the correct size and detail.

The nostrils are a difficult area. Burn a slot on both sides with the burning iron, then drill through from each side with a very small drill, making an oval hole. Build up the nostril area with plumber's epoxy putty, which is formed while wet, and let dry overnight. Cut the serrations on the underside of the upper mandible with a wood burner. Use a large drop of five-minute epoxy for the nail. Take the same amount of time detailing the underside of the bill as you do the top. I usually detail the bill and sand it smooth before I glue the head on.

Final Shaping

The final shaping of the body is done with a knife. This is a process of going back and forth between specimen or mount, photographs, drawings, and the wood carving. As you work, you tend to change the body contours here and there, and the duck tends to evolve from numerous minor decisions made along the way. Generally the body is not exactly the same on both sides. A raised primary may alter the overlapping and height of the tertials. The twist or stretch of the neck may affect the shape of the breast. More speculum may show on one side, and the tail may even be spread unevenly. An absolutely symmetrical duck would put it in the category of decorative rather than realistic carving.

When the body is close to final form, it is sanded with rough, smooth, and then fine sandpaper. Even at this stage you may alter the shape slightly, or find you must add some plastic wood to an area. At this point, the head, bill, and eyes should be completely carved. Leave the neck thicker than is necessary. Now glue the head on. Screw it tight from inside if it is a hollowed out body. Because the glue joint, or actually the glue itself, will bubble when burned, cut a wedge with an irregular edge completely around the joint after the head has dried.

Figure A-9 Screw head together. Leave uneven space around joint.

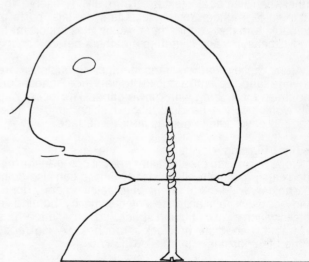

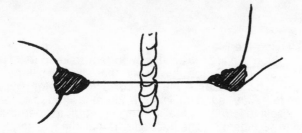

Fill with plastic wood.

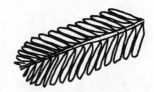

Hemlock (branch) Tree

Incorrect Burning

This wedge is filled with plastic wood, recarved, and sanded smooth. Make the plastic wood-basswood joint irregular around the neck, because it is easier to disguise an irregular line when burning the plastic wood at a much lower heat setting. At this point, the primaries and tertials are carved, but no other individual feathers have been defined. The wood is smooth, but not shiny.

After assembling all sketches, the mount or frozen specimen, and photographs, I begin to draw individual feathers and feather groups on the wood. Some of these will be brought into relief with a knife or chisel and some with a wood burner.

Correct Burning

Figure A-10 Draw in pencil lines showing direction of feather flow.

Gradually, a slight shingle effect begins to occur. Sand to bevel, and curve the edges to give a lumpy rather than fish scale texture. Normally, I reserve the outlining of feathers for the scapulars, tertials, parts of the back, and the side feathers. Again, it is important to study, measure, and sketch the feathers before carving them.

After these feathers and feather groupings are carved, sand the entire duck with very fine sandpaper, and finish by rubbing with brown paper. A grocery bag will work nicely. The duck should shine, and is now ready to have details burned into the surface.

Feather Burning

Wood burning to create feather detail can transform a good carving into a realistic piece of art. It can also point out the carver's lack of attention to detail if poorly done. Many carvers ruin an excellent carving by burning in details which are so stiff and structured that the feathers resemble Canadian hemlock branches. A correctly burned feather has curved, flowing lines.

To achieve these lines it is necessary to study feathers in detail. Sketch feathers on paper before burning them on the duck and take closeup photographs. Keep these photographs around when you are burning. It is as easy to burn correctly as it is to burn poorly. You must simply be aware of the structure and form of each feather you are burning.

I use two types of burning tools, the Hot Tool, a wooden-handled, constant temperature burning iron, and either the Feather Etcher or the Detailer, both of which are heat-regulated burners with knife-like burning tips. Beginning with the Hot Tool, burn the shafts of the obvious feathers: the tail, primaries, scapulars, tertials, some of the back feathers, and side feathers. On the longer exposed feathers, such as the scapulars and tertials. Touch the side of the Hot Tool to the feather at the shaft and pull back on each side to lower the wood, thereby raising the shaft. Now sand the shaft lightly to round it.

Figure A-12

Side View

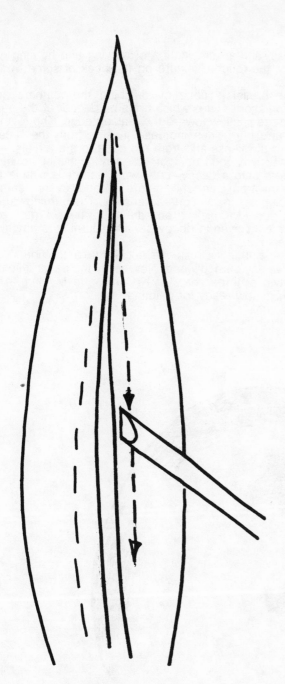

Top View

Next burn in random splits, drawing the Hot Tool from the edge of the feather in toward the shaft, curving it and lifting it as it nears the shaft.

Figure A-13

Touch Hot Tool to intersections of feathers and pull away. Sand feathers to bevel edges.

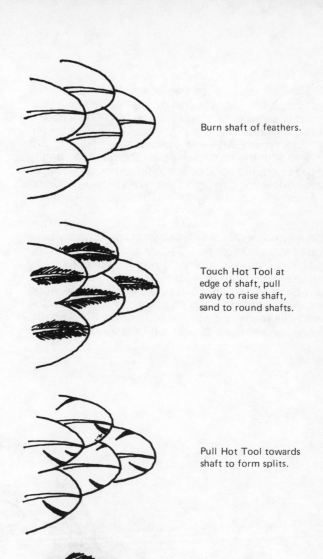

Burn shaft of feathers.

Touch Hot Tool at edge of shaft, pull away to raise shaft, sand to round shafts.

Pull Hot Tool towards shaft to form splits.

Use Feather Etcher or Detailer to burn fine lines.

Burning the splits first insures an even randomness and will prevent you from overdoing the splits. Larger ones, especially where the flank feathers meet the rump, are generally carved before they are burned. Do not use the Hot Tool on plastic wood areas, because it will melt and bubble.

After rechecking feather sizes and shapes, the bird is ready for fine line burning.

Fine Line Burning

Using a soft pencil, draw a few guide lines to designate the flow of the feathers and outline feathers which were not clearly defined by the Hot Tool. Then turn to the Feather Etcher or Detailer, which create an extremely fine line because they are knife-like regulated heat burners. These fine lines can be done with the Hot Tool, but I would suggest purchasing a heat regulated tool.

It is important to develop the technique of curving the lines slightly by twisting the pen as you pull it toward you. You must know where the line is going before you burn it so there is no hesitation when you touch the point to the wood. Experiment with the temperature settings, but never burn with the tip glowing red. The rule is to gently score the wood, not set it on fire. You will be surprised at how accurately you can burn lines. With experimentation and practice, your degree of realism will grealy increase.

During burning, carbon will build up on the point. Turn the burner off every few minutes and wipe it gently over a piece of 400 silicon paper. Carbon also builds up in the burned lines. This is brushed out with an old toothbrush. Do not use steel wool or a large brush.

Many different textures can be created with the wood burner. Just dabbing the tip on the wood will create the fine, hair-like feathers on the head near the bill. Longer, twisting lines are used on the top of the head and the cheeks, and a combination of carving and burning will create the rougher texture on the neck of some of the ducks.

The breast is done by outlining the feathers and burning shorter lines which are a bit deeper at the back and more shallow toward the leading edge. The feather size and burn lines increase in size from the breast toward the flanks and from the cape to the tertials.

It takes a good deal of time and patience to burn feathers onto a decoy, but every feather is a little bit different from the one before it and every feather grouping has its own characteristics. The burning varies from duck to duck, from drake to hen. When you become involved in decoy carving, burning is anything but tedious.

After burning, brush the duck with a toothbrush to remove any burned wood. Now spray the carving lightly with two or three coats of Krylon Matte Medium. The decoy is now ready for painting.

Figure A-14   FEATHER BURNING

34

Painting

My first five or six ducks were painted with oil paints. I switched to acrylics after finding that although blending was somewhat harder, the ease of preparation and use, drying time, and flexibility of the medium far outweighed the blending problems.

After buying several books on color, I decided to make my own paint chart using the colors normally found on ducks. The basic layout of colors is as follows:

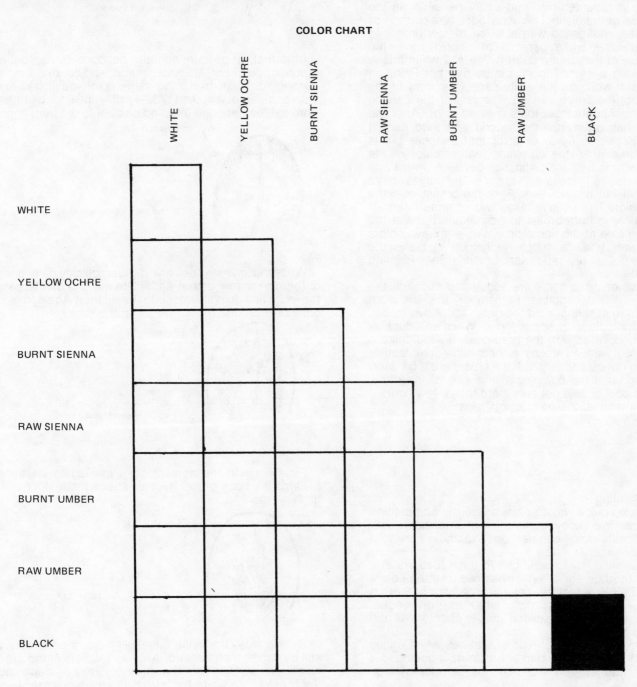

COLOR CHART

Figure A-15

Each square is painted with equal portions of the intersecting colors. The resulting chart gives you a good starting point to match to the actual feather. Then lighten, darken, or tint with a third color as required.

Painting the Base Coat

I paint the entire duck using three or four different brush sizes. Because we are painting on textured wood, the paint brushes wear out quickly. Never throw them away: They come in handy for stipple blending and texturing putty. I use white paper plates as paint pallets. Because painting a particular duck may stretch over a period of weeks, I do not premix colors.

Before beginning, go back to photographs and the specimen or mounted bird and lightly pencil in all the basic areas where distinct color changes take place. For white areas, mix gesso with a touch of raw umber to tone down the white. The paint should have the consistency of thin cream paint with a #12 white bristle brush, taking care not to fill the burn lines. Paint an undercoat of white on the white parts (feathers) of the carving, not the entire carving. The rest of the carving gets an under coat closer to its finished color. After the first coat has dried, paint a second and third coat if needed. Basically, try for a color that matches but is slightly darker than the dominant feather color of the area. If there is a sharp distinction between breast and side feathers, as there is with many of the drakes, paint an irregular but distinct line. Paint the breast with the darkest color. This usually takes two or three coats. If there is a blend from breast to side feathers, paint the breast and side at the same time. While the two colors are still wet, I use a stipple technique to blend the borders with a dry #6 sash brush. (See Painting Techniques.)

After two or three coats are added and stippled, the blend is usually acceptable. Remember, this is still an undercoat. In stippling, hold the brush about two inches away and stipple with some force. When the duck is completely covered with the base coat, it should like a well painted working decoy without individual feather colors. Do not be concerned if the colors are a bit dark. Depending upon the complexity and size of the duck, your base coat should not take more than a few hours if you have matched the paint colors closely.

Feather Painting

There is no quick way to paint a realistic competition grade decorative decoy, so time is not a consideration. Artistic quality and competition exactness are the principal criteria.

When painting, try to paint one to three feathers at a time, and assume each feather has two or three colors in it. Even a black feather may become gray further up the shaft, and may also have white or gray edges. Painting a single feather several shades of color will add depth and realism to it.

If we take a theoretical feather that has white edges and light brown fading to darker brown as it goes under the next feather, the following is a step-by-step procedure.

First, outline the leading edge with white and a touch of raw umber using a #1 or #2 sable brush. Do not attempt to blend the line. It is a simple stripe across the burn lines.

Figure A-16

1. Outline edge of feather with light stripe. Let dry.

This first stripe can actually be done on an entire group of feathers at once, as it should dry before continuing. Next, using the same color, paint hair-like lines of different lengths (1/32-1/16''), pulling the brush from the feather edge into and parallel to the burn lines.

Figure A-17

2. Use same color, stroke towards shaft.

While these white lines are still wet, quickly paint lines of the darker raw umber and white mixture overlapping the white and going further into the feather. Again, this is done only on one or two feathers at a time.

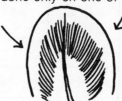

Figure A-18

3. While light color wet, stroke darker color in overlapping light.

Finally, using the darkest color and again brushing towards the back of the feather, shade the feather with its last color.

Figure A-19

4. Stroke darkest color into center of feather.

By this time, the white edge will have dried and may still be darker then desired. After all feathers in the area have been painted with the three colors, I go back and dry brush more white back from the leading edge. Use the #1 brush. Dip it in a creamy mixture, then wipe it off on a cloth. Stroke the small amount of color remaining as was done in the second step. (See Painting Techniques.)

36

Figure A-20

5. Paint splits, touch up, wash if necessary.

This process may have to be repeated several times, depending on the painter's talents and the complexity of the feather. If the entire feather is too light, just wash a watery raw umber over the area. Use very little paint. The wash can be applied as many times as is necessary to build up the right shade. If the feather is too dark, do not wash with white. That will cloud your paint job and change the color. It would be better to dry brush more strokes of light color into the feather. Next, shade the splits and deeper burned areas by pulling the darker color from the feather below through the white edge of the feather using a tempera technique. (See Painting Techniques.) This will break up the first white stripe painted many coats ago. Do not use black to make splits. Remember, the dark areas represent the color from the feather below.

The next step is to paint the shaft of the feather and add gloss to it. Use half water and half Liquitex Gloss medium to provide the shaft with a light sheen. Do not gloss the feather. The last step is to paint the remaining 599 feathers in the same manner! As a first choice, a bufflehead hen would be a good duck on which to practice blending, because the side feathers and breast require a good deal of work, while less work is needed on the top of the duck and on the head. The green winged teal hen is a small duck that requires quite a bit of feather blending. You will find that each duck presents its own painting problems and challenges.

Iridescence and Vermiculations

True iridescence of a duck's speculum is probably impossible to duplicate. You can take a green winged teal's wing and turn it in the light and it will appear blue. A mallard's blue speculum can appear purple. The best we can do is use the most often reflected color. "Rub and Buff" is an oil based powder in a small tube, available in many colors, that can be applied with fingers or brush to the appropriate areas. Because it is oil base, acrylics cannot be used on top if it. For this reason I prefer the iridescent acrylic paints. They are acrylic paints with tiny metal flakes which actually reflect the light. The metal flakes are whitish, so they tend to show up if used in excess. I mix the iridescent paint with regular acrylics to get the color I need, then apply the mixture to the area.

Realistic vermiculation is difficult to achieve. I have tried various types of marking pens, pen and India ink, and brush. I finally settled on acrylic paints and a very small brush, because of the waterproofing problems and the problems of color matching. The vermiculation pattern is difficult in itself because each feather has a particular pattern, and feathers underneath show through with their own pattern. Paint the light area as an uneven light or dark gray, then add the tiny dark vermiculations stroke by stroke. Many ducks, such as the scaup hen, have tiny dots on their feathers, which I also add with a very small brush.

Finishing

When the duck is finished, I check it over and usually find another half hour's painting to be done. It is amazing how a very thin wash of raw umber over the entire bird will sometimes tie everything together. This is not a standard procedure. Once in a while I find an area that should have a sheen to it. In such a case, water down some gloss medium and apply it in light strokes.

Coat the bottom with a few more coats of gesso, and label, sign, and date the carving so that it can be covered with tape if necessary for competition. I am not at all superstitious, but I wrap all my ducks in blue towels when I take them to contests. Not all my ducks wrapped in blue towels have won blue ribbons. But all of my ducks that have won blue ribbons have been wrapped in blue towels.

VERMICULATIONS ON A SCAUP

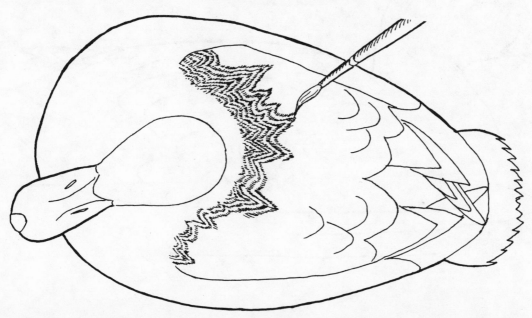

PRODUCING A SALEABLE CARVING

by
George Barber

Selecting the Project

My considerations in selecting a carving project are often predetermined by the number of orders I have for a specific carving. For the purpose of this writing I eliminated that pressure. Here, my only objective was satisfying the goal of producing a saleable carving. not a competition piece.

Determining the Type of Duck to Carve

A major consideration is how much time the project will take. The price of a carving can be controlled by supply and demand, or by production time. As a general rule, the larger the duck, the greater the production time required. During the period of working on this project, my time was limited to about 25 hours. There are two carvings in my series that fall in that time frame; namely, the green winged teal and the bufflehead. Since the green winged teal is one of my best sellers, I decided as a change of pace to do a bufflehead.

Selecting a Pose

With only 25 hours to complete the project, spread wing poses are out of the question; floating poses are the only considerations. The types of floating poses that may be considered are: (a) normal, (b) alert, (c) relaxed, (d) sleeper, (e) drinking (head projecting forward and downward), and (f) preening. Normal and relaxed poses are my best sellers, so I decided to do a normal pose. The following figures are outlines of various ducks representing each of the above poses.

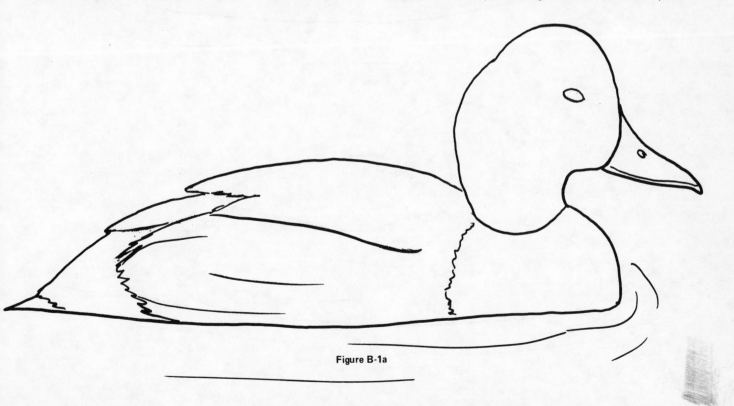

Figure B-1a

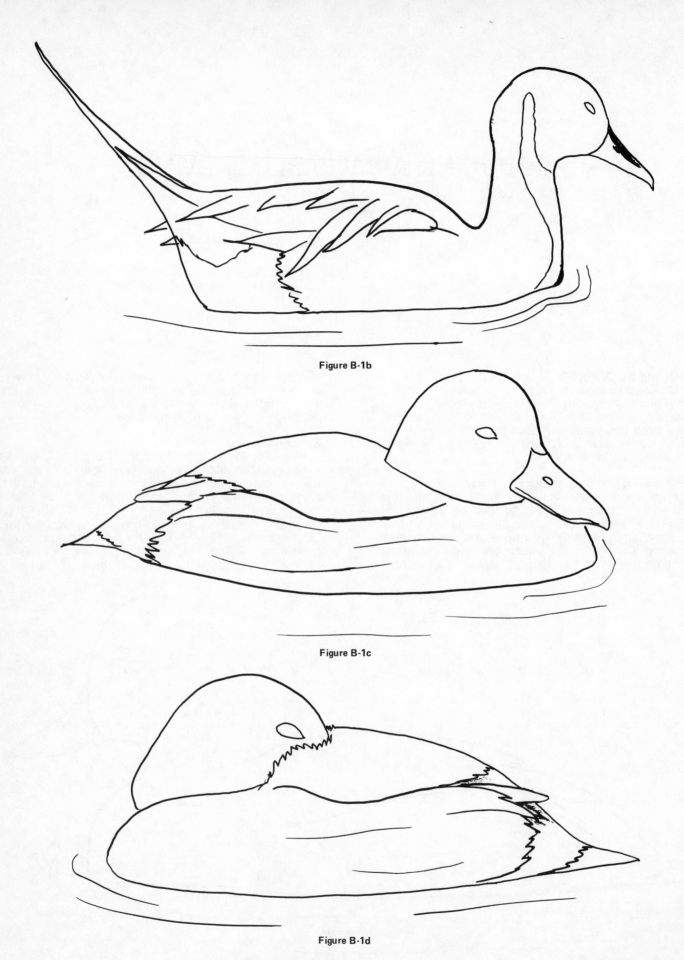

Figure B-1b

Figure B-1c

Figure B-1d

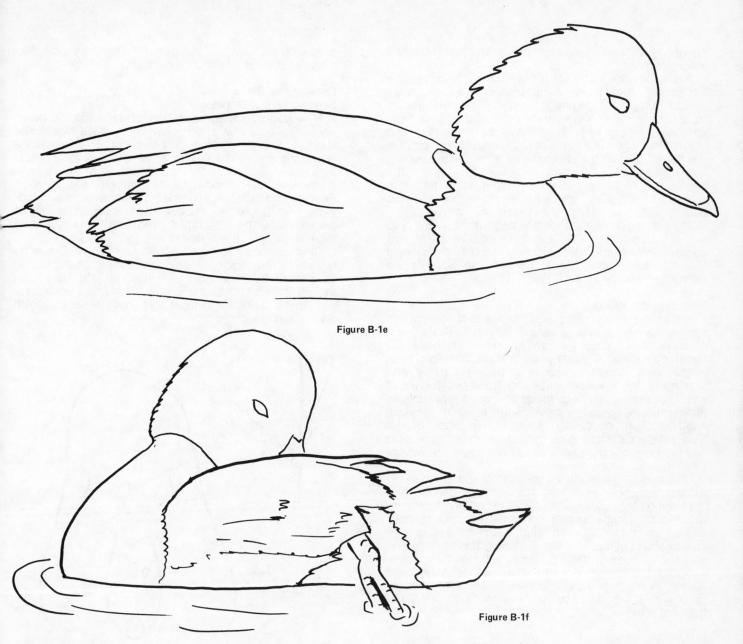

Figure B-1e

Figure B-1f

The Pattern

Once the type of duck and pose have been decided, you need a pattern. There are many sources of good patterns. The best I have found is photographs of an actual duck. Such photographs can be obtained at your local zoo if you have one in your area. In the absence of a zoo, photographs can be purchased at most large carving shows. Books are another source of such photographs.

Wildlife art shows that focus on carvings, such as those put on by the Ward Foundation of Salisbury, Maryland, are another major source of pattern information. The Ward Foundation is one of the leading organizations promoting the art of carving. It has both a Spring show which is usually held in Ocean City, Maryland during the last week in April; and a Fall show which generally takes place in Salisbury, Maryland during the second week in October. All serious carvers should join and support the Ward Foundation, Salisbury State College, Salisbury, Maryland 21801.

When you go to a wildlife art show, take your camera and shoot: (1) a side profile; (2) a top shot showing the back pattern; (3) a head profile; and (4) head on: from the bill to tail showing the width of the head and body. With these shots, you have a number of patterns and variations of patterns. To ensure proper proportions, put a six inch ruler in the first profile shot. For these shots use a 35mm camera with color slide film. I use 400 ASA with the proper filter for the light source. The speed film allows me to shoot indoors without a flash, which elminates the "hot spots" that obliterate the fine details.

Once you have studied a number of these photographs, you will discover that the differences between basic outline patterns for each species is slight. If there were large variations in basic patterns then it would be difficult to identify a specific duck. Simply put, all mallard drakes in breeding plumage look alike.

Still another source of patterns is the professional blank. A well designed professional blank gives the

41

carver a wealth of information and is an ideal reference for proportions.

A combination of all of these sources provides the carver with the reference material to draw the basic outline pattern for cutting his blank. The photographs from the wildlife art show can be projected on paper and the basic proportions (length from breast to tail and height from water line to top of back) are marked out. On this paper, project the photographs from the zoo (actual floating ducks), adjust the picture to within the boundaries of the proportioned marks, and trace an outline. Now study the various poses in all your photographs and adjust your outline accordingly.

There is a simpler way to obtain a pattern, which is to buy a pattern book. An excellent pattern series for competition or fine art production is William Veasey's ''Blue Ribbon Pattern Series'' which can be obtained from most wildlife book dealers.

Selecting the Wood

With the project and pose decided and the pattern drawn, the next step is to select the wood. There are 3 principal woods used for carving ducks: (1) bass, (2) tupelo gum, and (3) sugar pine. Without question, bass is the most popular because it makes carving and burning easier. However, I use very little bass. It is a soft wood, therefore, carvings made of it are susceptible to bump bruises. Since my carvings are for sale, they are handled often, especially at shows. Because of the frequent handling, carvings that are intended to be sold need to be more durable. For this reason, I use mostly sugar pine and tupelo gum.

On small ducks, such as the teals and bufflehead, I will use pine not only for its strength (it is denser than bass or soft tupelo), but also for its wood grain pattern, which adds another dimension to the finished carving. The grain is visible even after painting. I also use combinations of tupelo and pine, tupelo for the body and pine for the head. Tupelo comes in soft, medium, hard, and rock hard, so make sure you know what you are buying. A medium tupelo makes a fine body that will burn evenly, yet have sufficient strength to withstand frequent handling.

Making the Blank

Making the blank is a two part process. It involves cutting the outline with a bandsaw and grinding (drum sanding) down to the blank. In the first step I make maximum use of the bandsaw. I cut the outline and to the extent possible use the bandsaw for trimming. It is at this point in the process that the professional blank is used. (See section on Equipment.) First I mark my center line from bill to tail, and cut away large chunks, using the reference blank to compare with and mark the high spots. Studying and marking the high spots with care is a necessity. Once you have marked a spot, turn the rough cutout and the reference blank to another position to ensure that you have marked the right place. When you are close to your final shape, use the drum sander.

For drum sanding I use a homemade 2 and 1/2 inch drum sander. I use much the same technique with the drum sander as I did with the bandsaw. Compare the professional blank to your blank and mark the parts to be sanded accordingly. The process is quick, and has

produced excellent results for me. To produce a blank of a bufflehead takes about two hours.

Carving the Blank
Starting with a Drawing

Now go to your workbench and begin with the head. My basic technique at this point is to use a pencil and short blade carver's knife, in that order. Ensure that the centerline is well defined, and then draw as much detail as you can, including depressions which are represented by shading. Spend a lot of time with the drawing. Refer to photographs and reference tools such as study skins and the resin cast bill. (See Tool section.) The more precise the drawing, the more flair and character the finished piece will have.

On my duck's heads you will find eyebrows. Ducks do not have eyebrows; but I feel it gives them character, so I put them on. On a scaup I will exaggerate the size of the bill, making it broad and bold. This takes advantage of nature's design and highlights those features which distinguish the duck.

Epoxy Putty

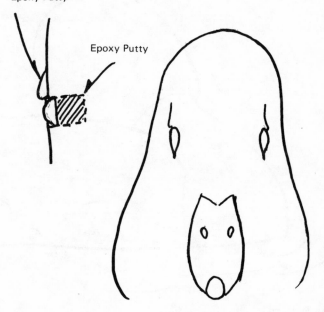

Epoxy Putty

Figure B-2

Back to the bufflehead. With this duck, you want to project an air of softness and delicacy. To accomplish this I concentrate on shaping the eyes and head contours accordingly. The eyes go in later, so for now concentrate on the contours of the head. The area behind the eye should be grooved, but the groove should be gradual and blend in with the head. The cheeks should be distinctive, but not bulging. For example, in a redhead you will have large puffed out cheeks, giving a bold appearance. Since you want just the opposite effect, control the depression so it is gradual and blends with the cheeks and head ridge. Your photographs of heads, which you should have taken at previous art shows, can now be used to compare degree of depressions. This will be seen on the shots taken from bill to tail, head on.

FRONT PROFILE

Up to now you have only used a pencil, heavily shading the areas where wood is to be removed. When you are done with the drawing, you should have a two dimensional drawing on a three dimensional object. Study the drawing very carefully. It is representative of the final product. If you do not like what you see, there is little sense in continuing. Redraw the head first. If you still do not like the effect, recut the head blank, probably in a different pose. It is essential that you be satisfied with the drawing.

Removing Wood From The Head

Beginning with the bill, remove wood, constantly referencing the resin cast bill. If during the process you obliterate the centerline, stop and reestablish it. With the bufflehead, do not worry about exaggerating the bill; your goal is accuracy. One option is to use a Foredom tool for the entire job, but I personally prefer a knife for the initial carving. A knife removes a lot of wood in a short time, and I find it more accurate then the Foredom. After the initial cuts, the drawing is obliterated and needs to be redone. The second time, do not draw the details. Simply outline them so you can continue carving. Continue this process until you are ready to smooth the surface; that is when you are near the finished shape. Now use the Foredom and a sanding drum to eliminate the "cut" lines. The sanding drums are small metal cylinders impregnated with grains of synthetic ruby on the outer surface. These drums are available from various dealers at art shows. They do an excellent job, and last a long time.

The finishing touch, before burning and adding detail, is to use sandpaper, 300 and 400 grit, to smooth the surface as much as possible. After sanding you are ready to complete the bill. An examination of the resin cast bill shows a number of imperfections on its surface. The bill of a duck has ridges, normally around the nostrils, and all ducks have a groove, and corresponding ridge, around the circumference of the maxilla (upper bill). Take an old dental tool, either a pick or scraper, and press its point or edge into the wood of the bill to add the grooves and ridges, using the resin bill as a guide. Throughout this process make extensive use of rifflers. Their odd shapes and fine sanding effects are excellent for smoothing the edges of grooves or adding grooves. Another way to fashion the ridge along the circumference of the maxilla, is to first draw a line representing the groove and then, using a burner on low heat, burn in the groove. After burning, use a folded piece of 300 grit sandpaper or a riffler to smooth the burn line and blend the groove to the bill. This creates a rounded ridge.

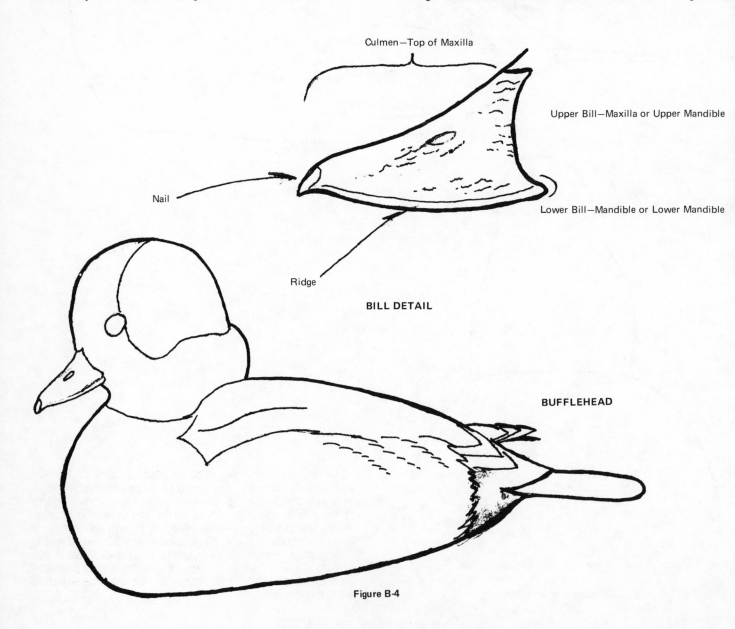

Culmen—Top of Maxilla

Upper Bill—Maxilla or Upper Mandible

Nail

Lower Bill—Mandible or Lower Mandible

Ridge

BILL DETAIL

BUFFLEHEAD

Figure B-4

44

The nostrils also present special problems, the first of which is to locate the center of the nostril on each side of the bill. Do this by comparing the resin bill to the carving. Make a mark on the culmen at the center point of the nostil. Then put tape around the bill with one edge against the mark. Holding the resin cast in one hand and the head blank in the other hand, look straight down the bill with them side-by-side, sighting the level of the nostril on each side. After both sides are marked, check, and adjust accordingly. After the nostrils are marked and drawn, use the Foredom with a "flame" bit to drill them out. On most ducks, I will drill through to the opposite side so you can look at a bill profile and see light from the other side.

With the bill complete, take a small drill on the Foredom and drill the center of the eye holes. This small drill will be a guide for the larger 8mm drill used for the eye hole. I normally do not drill through the head, but only make a shallow eye hole. When I use glass eyes on wire, however, I drill the guide hole to the other side so the eyes can be pushed out if needed. The head is now ready for burning. I place the eyes in just before painting, and some times even afterward. The next step is to prepare the body, burn in the feathers on both the head and the body.

Carving the Body

Before actually removing wood, you have a number of decisions to make, among which are: what type of feather pattern to use; how much of the secondaries and speculum, if any, to show; and whether to use feather inserts, or carve the primaries from the blank, or do both.

The Body Feather Pattern

To attempt an exact duplicate of nature's design would be a difficult and extremely time-consuming task. Most carvings are conceptions of what the pattern looks like. For example, on most carvings you can distinguish between scapulars, tertials, and back feathers. On a real bufflehead such a distinction is not possible. To determine what feather pattern to use is a matter of preference. For those who have not developed a pattern, I would recommend studying the following sources: photographs from art shows, study skins, photographs in books, and paintings of the duck. All of these will give you ideas. Choose those that suit your esthetic tastes and draw the results on the blank body. Always keep in mind how the feathers look on the actual duck, and what feather tract they grow in. Knowing where the feathers grow gives your carving a natural look. Having your feathers lay like rows of corn adds rigidity to your art piece and removes the resemblance to its living counterpart. (Reference section on Feather Structure.)

BACK PATTERN FOR A GREEN WINGED TEAL

Figure B-5

There is one other technique in drawing a pattern that is used by professional ornithology-taxidermists to enable them to arrange the feather pattern on a mounted specimen more accurately. I have, on occasion, used this technique with excellent results. It is not part of my normal process, because of the time it consumes. The technique involves drawing an outline of the pose, which you should have from your blank pattern, and then drawing the bird's skeleton inside the outline. Once this is completed, the feather tracts are marked and arrows are drawn from the tracts showing the direction the feathers lay on the duck. This drawing is used as a guide when drawing your feather pattern on the blank.

Again, make sure you are satisfied with the drawing. If it does not satisfy you in pencil, it probably will not satisfy you when it is carved. I have found that drawing the centerline on the body and drawing half a pattern saves time. If the half pattern does not look good, do it over again until you are satisfied; then do the other half.

On the bufflehead I decided not to show any of the secondaries and to use bass wood inserts for the primaries. Such decisions should be transfered to the body with a pencil. As with the head, take time to do a detailed drawing, including adding shading where you want to remove the most wood. With a short blade carving knife, remove wood from the shaded areas. Replace the detail drawing with an outline as it is obliterated. Also use the carving knife to relieve the tertials; this method is exacting but touchy. When using a knife to relieve the scapulars and tertials, a shallow cut is made following the drawing line. The second cut again follows the drawing line at as close to a ninety degree angle as you can get the knife and about 1/32 of an inch deep or less. These feathers can also be brought into relief with a heavy burning iron. Sand the edges of the burn to blend it to the body. Try the knife. It takes more practice, but is worth the effort.

When you have completed carving, return to the Foredom tool and sand the cut marks. The folds that were drawn on the side feathers will now be grooved with a carbide rasping bit. Once all the grooves are added, resort to 300 grit sandpaper, jewelers files, and/or rifflers for smoothing the surface to eliminate any remaining cut marks or undesired irregularities.

Texturing the Blank

The final technique I use before burning in the feather pattern is texturing the surface. This is done with a specially prepared carbide rasping bit on the Foredom. The bit has a ¼ inch shank. When you first purchase the bit, run it against a carbide disk. I use an old cinder block cutting disk to dull the carbide spikes and make them even. Then lightly touch the bit to the surface of a piece of pine and examine the texture. If the rasp marks are uneven or sharp, dull the bit again and retest it. Getting the bit just right is a slow process. Take your time, carbide bits are expensive. Always wear eye protection when grinding. A carbide chip in your eye can do a lot of damage.

Once the bit is prepared, texture the portions of the duck that do not show a defined feather. Most portions of the head, neck, breast, side feathers, the higher portions of the back and rump, and the under tail coverts are textured. Before beginning, draw guide lines on the wood in the direction of the feathers. With the prepared rasping bit in the Foredom, lightly touch the wood in a sweeping motion, following the direction of the drawn lines. This leaves a very fine raked surface on which you lay burn marks. This technique works well on pine and tupelo gum. It does not work well on bass, which has a tendency to shred. Practice texturing on scrap wood before trying it on a carving. It is a difficult technique to master. Practice the technique until you've mastered it so you don't destroy a good carving. In spite of the difficulty, this is a good technique to learn, because of the soft, delicate quality it adds to your carving. This technique can also be accomplished with a rasper (a sculpturing tool) if you do not have a Foredom.

Burning the Head Feathers

I am now about 10 hours into the project. The bufflehead is carved, the feather pattern is relieved, and the surfaces are textured. It is now time to burn in the feathers. Using a burning tool is an art in itself. If you do not believe this, just watch masters of this art, such as George Walker, a premier east coast carver, whose son invented the "Feather Etcher." A burning tool in George's hand becomes a creative artist's instrument. George has years of experience and practice behind each stroke he makes with the burning iron. I know of no quick, easy method to acquire this expertise. It is a matter of practice and experimentation. I also believe that with normal eye-hand coordination, practice, and patience you can master any and all burning techniques.

On the bufflehead, begin by burning the head feathers. Burn an overlapping arch pattern, beginning at the top of the culmen and fading out at the back of the crown. Once this pattern is burned, draw guide lines for the remaining head burns. In short burn strokes, burn the remainder of the head. The short burn strokes should have an overlapping random pattern.

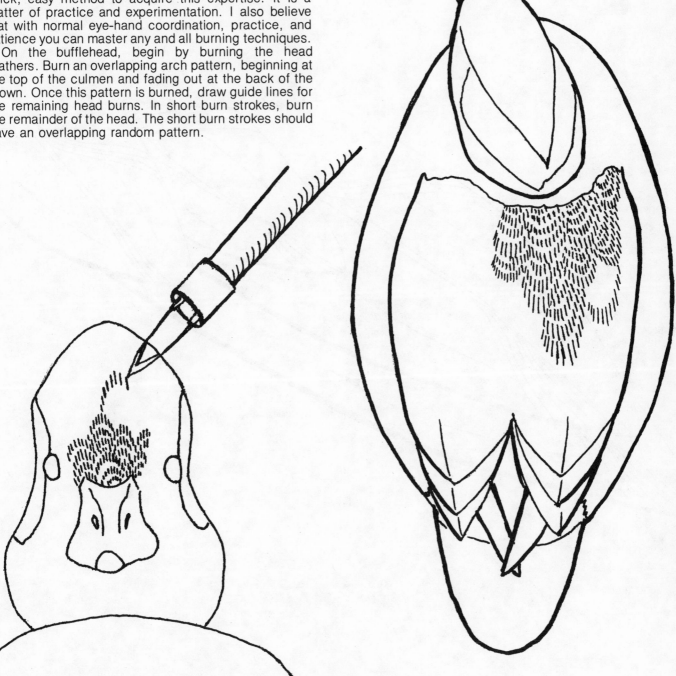

Figure B-6

ARCH BURN PATTERN

Burning the Body Feathers

On the body, I start by burning the ribs of any defined feathers. I start at the tip of the feather and burn toward the base. My lines for the ribs are not parallel, but are more like a long tapered spear that is curved to suggest a natural lay. After burning all the ribs, I burn the barbs. I always work from left to right, curving the barbs and decreasing the angle in relation to the rib as I get closer to the tip.

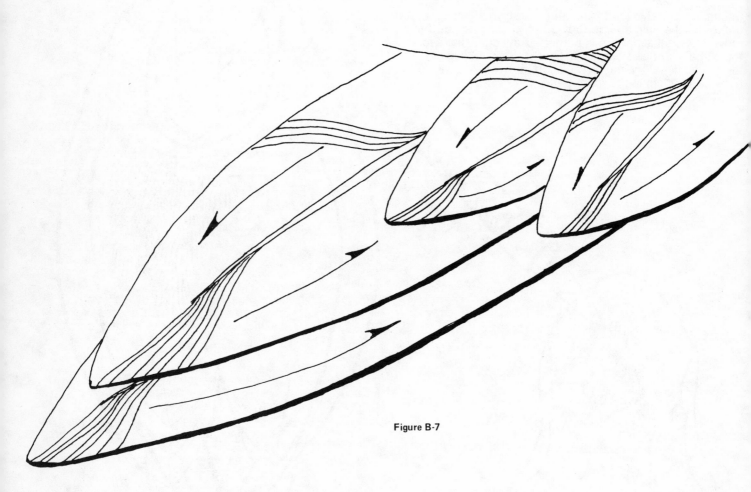

Figure B-7

Burning Split Feathers

Before burning the barbs, decide which feathers, if any, should have splits. Draw in all the splits. After they are drawn in, study the carving to ensure that the splits will have a random appearance. Once you are satisfied, burn the barbs.

Miscellaneous Burning Techniques

By changing the burning tip (there is a variety of tip shapes you can make or purchase), you can burn any desired shape. Varying the burn shapes can add creativity and originality to your carving. I use three principal shapes: (1) arrow shaped with sharp edges, (2) spade shaped with dull edges, and (3) "L" shaped with a point. I use the first one the most; it does all of my feather burning. Number two is used when burning in a depression; it appears to give the depression more definition. Number (3) is used to relieve the "V" notch where individual feathers or group of feathers meet.

Figure B-8

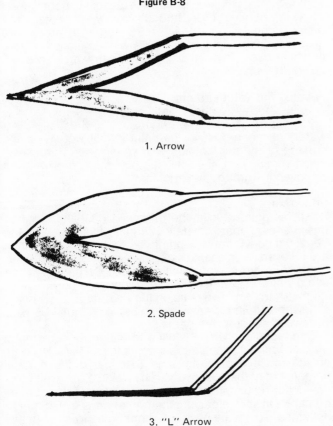

1. Arrow

2. Spade

3. "L" Arrow

When burning, keep the edge of the tip sharp by stropping it against a piece of very fine emery cloth.

Assembling the Parts

Once the burning is complete, the parts (the head and body) are assembled. We have not yet discussed the primaries, which I do after I paint. This admittedly is backward, but that is the way I do it. Use a product called Titebond Wood Glue to glue the head on. Blend the head to the body using epoxy putty. The putty is inexpensive, and can be worked with a Foredom grinding bit when set. I prefer to work the putty while it is still wet. It stays wet for at least 30 minutes and works well with water, like clay. Smooth the putty over the joints and use a sharp knife to press in simulated burn marks. Once the putty is textured with the knife marks, wet your fingertips and resmooth the edge, making the edge thinner. Now texture the edge again. The more time you take with this process, the less visible your joint will be.

The Final Touch

Once the glue and putty have dried, finish this part of the process by lightly sanding the duck with an abrasive fabric, which can be obtained from many of the suppliers listed in the Retailers section. Then, using a camel hair circular brush on the Foredom, lightly brush the entire duck. This brushing cleans out loose particles in the burn marks. The duck is now ready to seal.

Preparing to Paint

One of the important steps in painting is the preparation, especially if you are using acrylic paints. Acrylics are water based, so it is necessary to seal the carving to prevent the wood from swelling. A quick method of accomplishing this is to spray the duck with Krylon 1303, one of a number of commercial clear acrylic sprays. After spraying, allow at least 15 minutes drying time, and give it two more coats. Each coat should be light; a heavy coat will clog the delicate burn marks.

A more time consuming process which gives better results , was given to me by George Walker. (See "Feather Etcher" in "Burning the Blank") George's technique is to use 40% to 50% acrylic lacquer mixed with 50% to 60% acrylic lacquer thinner. The more thinner you use, the less likely you are to fill the delicate burn marks. Several coats are applied, waiting a *reasonable period* (approximately 30 minutes), between coats for thorough drying. The lacquer sealer not only seals the duck, but gives an excellent surface for the acrylic paint. Remember, the secret to any sealer is not to overdo it.

Color Information

The bufflehead is now prepared for painting. I have about 17 hours in the project. The next problem is to obtain color information. Photographs taken at art shows, in which the photographer has adjusted the source of light to accomodate the type of film used, are one of many good sources for color information. Such photographs are not difficult to take. Use a filter on your camera lens. Use color daylight slide 400 ASA film. Shop around; at discount stores like K-Mart you can save as much as 30% on film. In fluorescent light you need no filter. In tungsten or other artificial light sources use an 80A filter, which is dark blue. Because of the speed of the film, even with the filter, you will not need a flash to take excellent close-up pictures. Get as close to your subject as you can when you take pictures. Often I will take an extreme close-up showing the burning techniques. Take at least five shots of each of five different carvings of the same species. This gives you an opportunity to select the mean color (as oppose to the extremes). By using the mean color you should be fairly close to a representative color.

Another source of color information is books on carving. To be on the safe side never rely on one book as a source; check several and if they agree you should be safe in using their color scheme.

A riskier source of color information is the mounted specimen. There are many variables involved with the color of mounted birds. Principal among these are : the bird's food source; the time of year the specimen was taken; age of the specimen; the specimen's breeding population; and the specimen's health when taken. The method of taxidermy and the effects of light are also factors. If the specimen is old it was probably preserved with arsenic and has had considerable exposure to light. Arsenic, with time, may affect coloration. There is no dispute about the effects of ultraviolet light on coloration. If arsenic was not used, then a borax base preservative probably was. It is generally agreed that with time borax can change the colors of feathers. I was once doing a commissioned painting of an ivory bill woodpecker and needed a reference. Since the bird is probably extinct and I had never seen one, I went to the Smithsonian and viewed their museum mounts. In some of their specimens the brilliant red crest of the males had turned orange. This was the effect of light and/or preservatives. It explains why in a recent painting I had seen an orange crested ivory bill. The artist probably had only one specimen to reference, and that specimen's red crest had turned to orange. I strongly advise you not to depend upon a single mounted specimen for color information.

My wife, Bev, and I have been doing research for the last three years on the coloration of the order Anseriformes, family Anatidae (waterfowl). This research has been done at the Smithsonian's National Museum of Natural History, with its extensive collection and references. We started our research in an effort to write a paper on the coloration of the "soft parts" (the tarsus, bill, and iris). The soft parts change color approximately one hour after death and have to be reconstructed by taxidermists. This is why I have a male wood duck in breeding plumage with yellow eyes. (Unfortunately the taxidermist who did this mount did not have a good source of color information.) After we saw the quantity and quality of the research material available, we decided to expand our efforts to produce a reference text on the coloration of Anseriformes. Our goal is to describe the mean or average colors of the species and, where possible, to give basic color mixing for that reference. We hope to complete this reference text in 1984.

The colors for an adult male bufflehead are:

Soft Parts
Bill—Bluish, darker at the base where it is nearly blue. The blue color is called plumbeous (reference Ridgeway color standards of 1886). It is a mixture of cobalt blue, lamp black, and white.
Iris—Dark brown.
Tarsus—Light pink with darker joints (this is not part of this project).

Feather Colors
Head and Neck—With exception of white patch, the base color is mars black. On this base, place iridescent green on the anterior part of the head, the forehead, and between the eye and bill to the lower part of the bill. On the crown and cheeks, use iridescent purple. The white patch extends from behind the eye to the upper portion of the cheek, around the occiput to the other side.
Lower Neck, Breast, and Side Feathers—White.
Wing Coverts, Secondaries and Outer Scapulars—White.
Back Feathers, Inter-Scapulars, Tertials—Dull black.
Rump—BLack to ash gray (light gray and a touch of cobalt blue).
Upper Tail Coverts—Light ash gray.
Tail Feathers—Slate gray (black and white). I like to wash the slate gray with a thin wash of umber. The tail feathers' ribs are black.
Primaries—Dark umber (umber and black). Tinge the edges with burnt umber. The primary ribs are black.

Begin by painting the white parts. Use at least three coats (all thinned with at least 50% water) to ensure complete coverage. Now paint the black parts, again using three coats on to ensure coverage. Apply the paint with a flat, square brush that has stiff bristles and use a scrubbling technique. (Reference painting techniques.) Allow the carving to dry throughly between coats. After drying, check it carefully to ensure all areas are covered. Often, deep burn marks will remain unpainted, in which case, thin the paint more with water so it will flow into these crevices.

Painting the Tail Feathers
Paint the tail feathers slate gray. When this coat is dry, go over it with a watery coat (25% color, 75% water) of umber. While the paint is still wet, wipe the surface of the tail feathers with your hand. This leaves paint (umber) in the tail feather burn grooves but removes it from the high points.

Primaries
At this point, put in the primaries. Cut them out of bass veneer, approximately 1/8 inch thick. As with the head and body, draw the primaries first. The drawn lines are relieved (high on one side, low on the other) with the Feather Etcher equipped with a spade shaped tip. Then use a riffler or jeweler's file to smooth the burn marks. With a sharp, knife edge tip on the Feather Etcher, using a lower burning heat, remember you are burning basswood, burn in the barbs.

One technique which is used to make the duck more realistic without taking more time, is to use bass wood to do the top two primaries and then carve the bottom primary out of the base wood. The top two primaries are then inserted under the tertials but on top of the bottom primary. On such a carving the primary tips would meet, not cross. To get the bass wood primaries to cling to the body, soak them in water after burning and then tape in place (on the carving) to dry. Once dried, seal and paint them.

Shading
Two secrets to bufflehead painting are proper shading and iridescence. For shading use the techniques of stippling and tempera painting. Start with the lightest shades of gray and gradually increase the hue in successively smaller areas toward the darkest shade. I seldom use black for shading; I almost always use some shades of gray. The areas to be shaded are the shoulder joint area, the folds in the side feathers, the rump, the

leg slots, and the vent. After these areas are shaded with gray, thin yellow ochre paint with water (5% paint and 95% water). Streak the side feathers and the area behind the eye. While the paint is still wet, wipe it off with your hand. This decreases the intensity of the shading and helps blend it with the background paint.

Iridescence

I prefer to imbed the iridescent powder in a clear coat of gel medium. This is done by putting a dab of gel the size of a dime on your pallet and mixing it with an equal amount of water. Then with a wet #4 brush, dip the tip halfway into the iridescent powder. Mix the powder that clings to the brush with the gel and water mixture. Then fan the brush and lightly stroke against a paper towel to get rid of the excess on the tip. Now brush against (at a right angle to) the burn marks. This will leave a quantity of gel with suspended powder on top of the burn marks, rather than in the ridges. Allow to dry between coats, and repeat until you attain the desired degree of iridescence. This is a slow technique, but it is worth it.

Highlighting

Highlighting is a commonly used technique for eye appeal. My carvings are representations of floating ducks from the water line up, so I like to give the bills a wet appearance. To accomplish this, use a mixture of water and gel medium (30% water and 70% gel) to paint the maxilla. Three coats will give it a wet appearance. Be sure and allow drying time (15 minutes) between coats. The ribs of the tertials and scapulars can also be highlighted with the same technique.

Signing Your Carving

Personalizing a carving with your signature states that you feel it is a quality piece of art. A signature can be put on with ink, paint, burner, or branding iron. I use the latter.

SELLING - SHOWS - RETAILERS

Selling the Carving

At the beginning of this writing, I stated that my goal was to be a successful professional artist-carver. To me that means producing an art piece that patrons are willing to purchase. Fortunately, my carvings are in demand. In fact, at this writing I only have two carvings, the bufflehead for this project and the first carving I ever did, a green winged teal. The teal is not for sale, it is the rule by which I measure my progress.

There are a number of places to sell your carving. Each has its advantages and disadvantages. The principal sales areas are: fine art shows, arts and craft shows, craft shows, wildlife art shows, art galleries, frame shops, and gift/variety shops.

Wildlife Art Shows

Wildlife shows specializing in ducks, whether they are festivals, expositions, or shows, are my preference for art sales. The larger ones are well-planned, well-advertised events. Before you exhibit at such a show, consider the cost of exhibiting; the fee or commission charge; and most importantly, whether all exhibitors are treated equally.

Cost of Exhibiting

Transportation, food, and equipment, are expensive. Whether you sell or not you still must pay for food and lodging, so when you first start selling your work it may be best to consider local shows. After you gain confidence in your marketability, you can expand.

Fee or Commission

Most professional artists prefer to pay a fee rather than a commission (a commission being a portion or percentage of the sale price of the art). Some shows have both a fee and commission. If you are a beginner, then a commission is not bad as long as your sales are low. A large fee for a 1984 show would be $100 for an 8 foot space with table and pegboard. Compare this to a commission of 30%, the normal commission for large, organizer handled shows (shows where the artist delivers the art work and the organizers exhibit and sell it). It is not uncommon for artists to increase their prices to offset the commission at such shows. This means that the patron pays more for the same piece of art.

I would like to note that even though the Ward Foundation puts on one of the largest and best art shows on the Atlantic coast, it does not charge its exhibitors a fee or commission. Its objective is to promote the art of carving. At the fall show, which normally takes place in mid-October, you can purchase wildlife art at the best prices.

Treatment of Exhibitors

This is one of the most important considerations in deciding to do an art show for the second time. All art shows have rules. Unfortunately, some art shows do not apply the rules equally to all exhibitors. Insist upon equal treatment. There are too many shows to put up with anything less. Exhibitors should realize that without their support the show would not exist. Remember, you are paying the same amount as the top selling artist to display your work at a show. If you are not treated fairly, do not spend your hard earned money exhibiting.

Artist—Carver's Association

An artist-carver's association is sorely needed. If all semi-professional and professional artists belonged to an association like doctors (AMA) or lawyers (Bar Association), inequities in shows could be eliminated, and the sometimes exorbitant commissions and/or fees would be reduced.

Different types of Shows

Once you exhibit your work in places other than the wildlife art show, you greatly reduce the number of patrons interested in your medium. At the same time you reduce the competition. I know a very successful artist who has developed a following by doing mall art shows all over the country. He maintains a mailing list and virtually has a one man show wherever he goes. This takes time to develop but once developed provides a steady income.

Craft Shows

Most craft shows have very little to do with fine art. The average sale at such a show will be under $10. Check craft shows out carefully before you commit yourself.

Art Galleries

I exhibit work at art galleries from New York to Florida and from Washington D.C. to Carmel, California. The principal arrangement with these galleries is consignment. That is, I own the art piece and the gallery exhibits it; when it is sold, the gallery gets a commission, which is normally 30%. Galleries are very useful for exposure. The disadvantage is that you tie up a number of pieces that you could exhibit and sell.

Wildlife Art Show List

I have not listed shows that are large and have more exhibitors than they can handle, such as the Ward Foundation Shows. This should not discourage you from contacting such shows. Most have a waiting list and it may take a while to get a slot, but if you have patience you will be allowed to exhibit. The following shows are either beginning shows or regional and local shows. Most have carving contests. for either exhibition, sales, or competition, contact these shows. If you know of a show that you can recommend and it is not listed, write to me (George Barber, 4206 Knowles Avenue, Kensington, Maryland 20895) and I will include it in my next book. If you write and would like an answer, please enclose a self addressed, stamped envelope.

Wildlife Art Show List

Richmond's Annual Wildfowl Carving and
    Art Show
Sponsored by Northside Lions Club
Richmond, Virginia
(Usually held in February)

Havre de Grace Decoy Festival
P.O. Box A
Havre de Grace, Maryland 21078
(Usually held in May)

Fairfax County Part Authority Wildlife
    Art and Photography Show
4030 Hummer Road
Annandale, Virginia 22003
(Usually held in March)

Southeastern Wildlife Exposition, Inc.
Suite 24, 1316 Washington Street
Columbia, South Carolina 29201
(The first show was held in February in
Charleston)

Annapolis Wildfowl Carving and Art
    Exhibition
347 Elderwood Court
Annapolis, Maryland 21401
(The first show will be held in Januray)

Rappahannock River Waterfowl Show
Box 413
White Stone, Virginia 22578
(Usually held in March)

Bombay Hook National Wildlife Refuge
R.R. #1, Box 147
Smyrna, Deleware 19977
(Has exhibits from October to April)

U.S. National Decoy Show
5 Flint Road
Amity Harbor, New York 11701
(Held in March)

Meadowlands Wildfowl Festival
Waterfowlers of Bergen County
31 N. Demarest Avenue, New Jersey 07621
(Held in September)

Salem County Sportsmen's Club Show
Rt. 40
Deepwater, New Jersey
(Held in September)

Wings's Water Festival & Decoy Show
Wetlands Institute
Stone Harbor Boulevard
Stone Harbor, New Jersey 08247
(Held in September)

Currituck Wildlife Festival
Currituck Wildlife Guild
P.O. Box 91
Shawboro, North Carolina 27973
(Held in September)

Bird Carver Exhibit
Cape Cod Museum of Natural History
RR 1, Rte 6A
Brewster, Massachusetts 02631
(Held in September)

Louisiana Wildfowl Carvers & Collectors
    Guild Wildfowl Festival
615 Baronne Street
New Orleans, Louisiana 70113
(Held in September)

Decoy & Wildlife Show
Ocean City Recreation
P.O. Box 570
Ocean City, New Jersey 08226
(Held in September)

North Carolina Waterfowl Weekend
Outer Banks Chamber of Commerce
Attn: Waterfowl Information
P.O. Box 90
Kitty Hawk, North Carolina 27949
(Held in late September)

Yorkarvers Woodcarving & Decoy Show
728 Clearmount Road
York, Pennsylvania 17403
(Held in October)

Native American Wildfowl Woodcarving
    Workshop
Minnestrista Center for Non-Traditional
    Studies
400 Minnetrista Boulevard
Ball State University
Muncie, Indiana 47306
(Held in October)

Catahoula Lake Festival
P.O. Box 1782
Alexandria, Louisiana 71301
(Held in October)

Southern Wildfowl Festival
P.O. Box 46
Mooresville, Alabama 35649
(Held in November)

Bird Carving Show
Worcester Science Center
Harrington Way
Worcester, Massachusetts 01604
(Held in November)

Artistry in Wood Show
7014 Murray Lane
Annandale, Virginia 22003
(Held in November)

Long Island Wildfowl Carvers Competition
    and Show
8 Lynn Place
Bay Shore, New York 11706
(Held in December)

Pacific Southwest Wildfowl
9226 Lake Country Drive
Santee, California 92071
(Held in February)

Mid-Atlantic Wildfowl Festival
908 Abingdon Road
Virginia Beach, Virginia 23451
(Held in March)

Easter Decoy Festival
Chincoteague Chamber of Commerce
P.O. Box 258
Chincoteague, Virginia 23336
(Usually held Easter weekend)

California Open
Pacific Southwest Wildfowl Arts, Inc.,
731 Beech Avenue
Chula Vista, California 92010
(Usually held in February)

CARVING CLUBS

Capitol Area Wood Carvers Club
4068 Adams Drive
Wheaton, Maryland 20902

Retailers

*George Barber
4206 Knowles Avenue
Kensington, Maryland 20895
(Foredom Dealer & supplier of Mr. Duck-
The Learning Duck)

*Bob Miller
General Delivery
Evergreen, Louisiana 71333
(318) 346-4270
(Resin cast, waterfowl study bills)

*P.C. English Enterprises
Tr. 1, Box 136
Fredericksburg, Virginia 22401
(Large variety of supplies)

*Brookstone
127 Vose Farm Road
Peterborough, New Hampshire 03458
(Hard to find tools and supplies, rifflers
which are the size mentioned in the text,
epoxy putty, etc.)

*George Walker
Box 208 Chesterfield
Trenton, New Jersey 08620
(The Feather Etcher-a professional
burning tool)

*SETO Co. Inc.—Formerly H. Serabian
195 Highway 36
P.O. Box 146
West Keansburg, New Jersey 07734
(Special cutters, etc.)

Colwood Electronics
715 Westwood Avenue
Long Branch, New Jersey 07740
(The Detailer-a professional burning tool)

*Dolington Woodcrafts
Washington Crossing — Newtown Road
Newtown, Pennsylvania 18940
(Professional quality blanks)

Oscar Johnston Wildlife Gallery
Rt. 2, Box 1224
Smith River, California 95567
(Reference material)

The Decoy Factory
P.O. Box 60975
Rochester, New York 14606
(Wood supplier)

Christian T. Hummul Co.
Box 2877, Dept CT
Baltimore, Maryland 21225
(Large variety of items)

*Van Dyke's
Woonsocket, South Dakata 57385
(Taxidermy supplies, glass eyes, etc.)

Warren Tool Co.
Rt. 1, Box 14—AW
Rhinebeck, New York 12572
(Knives, etc.)

*Woodcraft
41 Atlantic Avenue
P.O. Box 4000
Woburn, Massachusetts 01888
(Large Variety of items)

*Ward Foundation Museum Shop
Salisbury State College
Salisbury, Maryland 21801
(Books)

*Books Plus
42 Charles Street
Lodi, New Jersey 07644
(Large variety of carving books)

*Carving Shop
RD 2, Forge Hill Road
Manchester, Pennsylvania 17345
(Wood & general supplies)

*Veasey Studios
955 Blue Ball Road
Elkton, Maryland 21921
(General supplies, pattern books, carving
and painting books)

Sears Roebuck and Co.
Source for drum sander and arbor
(described in text) for building your own
drum sander.

If I have left any retailers out, and I am sure I have, please write me and I will include you in the first revision of "Carving Techniques". Please, bonafide retailers of equipment or supplies only. Write your listing using the ones above as a guide. Only one line will be allowed for your name and what you supply. Artists, Carvers, and Gallery listings will not be accepted. I reserve the right to eliminate any listing without explanation. The principle reason for this listing is to give the intermediate or beginning carver a source from which to obtain material.

*These dealers I have dealt with and can recommend.

Index